Sarabel Kass Cohen
Georgia State University

D1278488

WORDS IN FOCUS

Building Reading Fluency

Maxwell Macmillan
INTERNATIONAL PUBLISHING GROUP
New York Oxford Singapore Sydney

Collier Macmillan Canada
Toronto

Library of Congress Cataloging-in-Publication Data

Cohen, Sarabel Kass.
    Words in focus : building reading fluency / Sarabel Kass Cohen.
      p.   cm.
    ISBN 0-02-323145-9
    1. English language--Textbooks for foreign speakers.   2. College
readers. I. Title.
PE1128.C685 1991
428.6'4--dc20
                                       90-5773
                                        CIP

Editor: Maggie Barbieri
Production Supervisor & Text Designer: Ros Herion Freese
Cover Designer: Sheree Goodman

This book was set in 11/13 ITC Berkeley Old Style Medium by Ruttle, Shaw & Wetherill, Inc., and printed and
bound by R.R. Donnelley & Sons. The cover was printed
by Lehigh Press.

Collier Macmillan Canada
1200 Eglinton Avenue, E.
Don Mills, Ontario, M3C 3N1

Printing: 1 2 3 4 5 6 7 Year: 1 2 3 4 5 6 7

Maxwell Macmillan
International Publishing Group
ESL/EFL Department
866 Third Avenue
New York, NY 10022

Printed in the U.S.A.

ISBN 0-02-323145-9

Reading Credits:
Ch. 1, pp. 2–3: Art Buchwald, "Daughter's 'Friend' Is a Boy," *The Atlanta Journal Constitution,* © 1977 Los Angeles Times Syndicate, Los Angeles, CA. Ch. 2, pp. 12–13: Jimmy Carter, *Why Not the Best?* (Nashville: Broadman Press, 1975), 16–18. All rights reserved. Used by permission. Ch. 3, pp. 24–25: Lewis Grizzard, "They Mourned Steve Vann in Silence," *The Atlanta Journal Constitution,* © 1989 Cowles Syndicate, Inc., reprinted with special permission of Cowles Syndicate, Inc. Ch. 4, pp. 34–36: Excerpt from *Kennedy* by Theodore Sorenson. Copyright © 1965 by Theodore C. Sorenson. Reprinted by permission of Harper & Row Publishers, Inc. Theodore C. Sorenson, *Kennedy as I Knew Him* (Kent: Hodder & Stoughton Limited). Ch. 5, pp. 46–47: *The Atlanta Journal Constitution.* Ch. 6, pp. 60–61: Excerpt from *Sylvia Porter's New Money Book for the 80's* by Sylvia Porter, copyright © 1975, 1979 by Sylvia Porter. Used by permission of Dou-
bleday, Dell Publishing Group, Inc. Ch. 7, pp. 66–68: "Dear Abby" letters, copyright © Universal Press Syndicate. Reprinted with permis-
sion. All rights reserved. "Ann Landers" letters, *The Atlanta Journal,* © Chicago Tribune, Chicago, IL. Ch. 8, pp. 76–78: Kirby W. Stanat with Patrick Reardon, *Job Hunting Secrets & Tactics* (Piscataway, NJ: New Century Publishers, Inc.), 102–107. Ch. 9, pp. 90–91: Richard Reeves, "American English: A World Language," copyright © 1983, Universal Press Syndicate. Reprinted with permission. All rights reserved. Ch. 10, pp. 98–100: Ellen Goodman, "The Soviet Superwoman," © 1985, The Boston Globe Newspaper Company / Washington Post Writers Group. Reprinted with permission. Ch. 11, pp. 110–111: Art Buchwald, "Don't Say 'Let's Get Together' to a Foreigner," *The Atlanta Jour-
nal Constitution,* © 1984 Los Angeles Times Syndicate, Los Angeles, CA. Ch. 13, pp. 118–119: Chet Fuller, "He Was as Easy for Me to Read as the Pages of an Open Book," copyright © 1988, *The Atlanta Constitution,* Atlanta, GA, June 27, 1988. Ch. 14, pp. 122–124: Ex-
cerpted from "President of the United States," *The World Book Ency-
clopedia* (Volume 15, 762–763, 766–767, 771). © 1989, World Book, Inc. Ch. 15, pp. 126–128: "Let's Get Personal," copyright © *The At-
lanta Journal and Constitution,* Atlanta, GA. Ch. 16, pp. 132–134: From *Our Marvelous Native Tongue: The Life and Times of the English Language,* by Robert Claiborne. Copyright © 1983 by Robert Claiborne. Reprinted by permission of Times Books, a Division of Ran-
dom House, Inc., and of the author. Ch. 16, p. 135: *Funk & Wagnall's Modern Guide to Synonyms.* Edited by S.I. Hayakawa. Copyright © 1968 by Funk & Wagnall's. Reprinted with permission.

Photo and Illustration Credits:
pp. 1 and 2 (Buchwald): Bill O'Leary / Permission granted for reprint. Distributed by the Los Angeles Times Syndicate. pp. 3, 91, and 124: Bill Keane, "The Family Circus." Copyright © 1977, 1978 King Features Syndicate. Reprinted with special permission of Cowles Syndi-
cate, Inc. pp. 1 and 12 (Carter): The Bettmann Archive. p. 13: Illus-
tration by Shelley Matheis. pp. 1, 34, and 36 (Kennedy): The Bettmann Archive. pp. 1 and 46: Aggie Lorenzo. pp. 61 and 113: "Dennis the Menace"® used by permission of Hank Ketcham and © by North America Syndicate. pp. 1 and 66 (Abigail Van Buren): Universal Press Syndicate. pp. 1 and 66 (Ann Landers): Chicago Tribune. p. 74 (Kudzu): By permission of Doug Marlette and Creators Syndi-
cate. pp. 1, 76, 109, 110, and 118: Eric Liebowitz. pp. 1 and 90: Lowell Reitchmuller. pp. 1 and 98 (Ellen Goodman): The Bettmann Archive. p. 100 © 1989 David Wink. p. 106: Mort Walker, "Beetle Bailey." Copyright © 1988 King Features Syndicate. Reprinted with special permission of King Features Syndicate, Inc. pp. 109 and 114 (Reagan): The Bettmann Archive. pp. 109 and 122 (Washington): The Bettmann Archive.

In memory of my parents
Ida and Charles Kass
and my brother
Irving Kass

Introduction

This reading and vocabulary text for pre-academic intermediate ESL students has two purposes: to develop reading fluency and to expand vocabulary.

It is obvious that motivation is essential to reading fluency and that without interesting texts, there is little motivation. My choice of reading selections for this text is based on my fourteen years' experience in the ESL classroom.

ESL students are particularly interested in the lifestyles and problems of their American counterparts: living together before marriage (Art Buchwald); drug abuse (Lewis Grizzard); budgeting in college (Sylvia Porter); getting a job (Kirby W. Stanat); meeting people of the opposite sex (personal ads). ESL readers enjoy human interest stories ("Desire for a Child Was Nearly Tragic"; letters to Ann Landers and Abigail Van Buren). They like humor ("Don't Say 'Let's Get Together' to a Foreigner"). They are interested in American government ("The Presidency") and recent Presidents of the United States (Kennedy and Carter). They are concerned with social issues (Ellen Goodman; Chet Fuller). And they want to know more about the English language (Richard Reeves; Robert Claiborne). The introductions to the readings give students an idea of the subject matter with which they will be dealing.

The text is in two parts: the first ten chapters and the remaining six. Both Part One and Part Two consist of authentic reading selections followed by various exercises and activities aimed at developing reading fluency and expanding vocabulary. However, Part Two is based on skills learned in Part One; that is, glossaries are furnished throughout Part One, whereas Part Two focuses on guessing meaning from context. The first ten chapters should be taught in sequence because of the explanations that accompany some of the word study exercises; the remaining chapters may be studied at random and may begin to be introduced after completion of Chapter 6.

The Exercises

READING COMPREHENSION

The reading comprehension exercises that follow each reading selection are aids in developing reading fluency. These exercises help readers recognize main ideas, focus on important details, and make necessary inferences; they include questions about the selections, true/false statements, and multiple-choice items. The interpretation exercises guide readers to a better understanding of the more difficult passages.

QUESTIONS FOR DISCUSSION

The discussion questions, based on the reading selections, are thought provoking and can lead to spirited exchanges about some rather controversial subjects. The discussions require students to relate their own experiences and attitudes to the reading. (Some of these questions can be used as a basis for pre-reading discussions.)

VOCABULARY DEVELOPMENT

Vocabulary development should not be left to chance; thus, much of this text is devoted to vocabulary study. Each of the first ten reading selections is followed by a list of the more difficult words in the selection; each word is defined and labeled a part of speech according to context. (In words of more than one syllable, the syllable of major stress is underlined.) The readings also serve as an excellent source for introducing and explaining idioms; compound words; words with multiple meanings; words used as different parts of speech; synonyms and antonyms; phrasal verbs; and words changed by prefixes and suffixes.

A wide variety of exercises, both written and oral, provides an opportunity for students to use the new vocabulary: choosing synonyms and antonyms; choosing appropriate words from a list to complete sentences; identifying the word that does not belong in a group; determining the appropriate meaning from context when a word has more than one meaning; completing conversations using phrasal verbs; recognizing inappropriate phrasal verbs in sentences; writing original sentences; guessing meaning from context, etc.

ACTIVITIES

The activities—role playing, writing a summary, writing an ending to a story, presenting mock job interviews, writing personal ads, participating in a vocabulary bee, etc.—offer a change of pace as well as further opportunity to use the new vocabulary.

COMIC STRIPS

The comic strips illustrate words and idioms in the text.

Acknowledgments

I wish to express my gratitude to Professor Becky Bodnar and Dr. Patricia Byrd for their many kindnesses. Professor Bodnar, my colleague at Georgia State University for fourteen years, encouraged me throughout the writing of *Words in Focus* and offered valuable suggestions. Dr. Byrd, chair of the Applied Linguistics/ESL Department at Georgia State, read the manuscript and made useful suggestions, shared with me her experience as a published author, and gave me her full support.

I would also like to thank Dr. Joan Carson, Georgia State University, and Sharon Salus, University of Maryland, for their review of and comments on the manuscript.

My further thanks go to the teachers and graduate students at Georgia State who used several of the first completed chapters of the text or the complete text in their ESL reading classes: Becky Bodnar, Fusun Ercan, Alice Gertzman, Susan Keenan, Phyliss H. Moir, Wendy Newstetter, Mike Oil, Poly Potter, and Peggy S. Wagner; and graduate students Carol Herrick, Vicki Safari, and Mike Thomas.

And, of course, many thanks to my delightful students at Georgia State, without whom there would be no book!

My gratitude to the editors and staff at Maxwell Macmillan International Publishing Group for their help: especially Maggie Barbieri, who worked with me and patiently answered my questions; Elizabeth Mirando, who advised about permissions; and Ros Herion Freese, production supervisor.

Finally, a very special thank you to my wonderful family—my husband, Gilbert; my sons, Kass and Seth; and my daughter, Pat—for their enthusiastic support.

S.K.C.

Contents

PART **ONE**

A humorist is a person who writes or tells funny stories. Art Buchwald is a well-known humorist. Through his syndicated newspaper columns,* he makes fun of American society, public officials in particular. In "Daughter's 'Friend' Is a Boy," he writes about a "problem" that some parents in the United States, and perhaps in your country, are having to face.

WASHINGTON—In the good old days when your daughter said she was bringing home a friend for the weekend, it meant she was bringing home a girl friend—and when your son said he was bringing
5 home a friend for the weekend, it was a boy.

This is not the case anymore, and it is causing tremendous houseguest problems throughout the country.

Since there is never any mention of the sex of the
10 friend on the phone, most parents don't know what to expect or how to handle it.

I was over at Ripley's house the other evening when his daughter, Joan, arrived home for the weekend with her "friend," a tall strapping fellow named
15 Mickey.

Mrs. Ripley was very flustered and said, "Well, Mickey, I guess you want to put your things away."

"Put them in my room," Joan said.

"Mickey can sleep in the attic," Mrs. Ripley said
20 nervously.

---

* *syndicated newspaper columns*: columns appearing in a number of newspapers at the same time.

"Why can't he sleep in my room?" Joan asked.

Mr. Ripley blew up. "Because I know he'd rather sleep in the attic."

"Joan's room is fine with me," Mickey said.

25 "Well, it isn't fine with me," Mr. Ripley snarled. "Mickey, do you mind if we talk to Joan alone? There's a beer in the ice box. Make yourself at home."

As soon as Mickey left the room, Joan said, "How could you humiliate me in front of my friend?"

30 "How did we humiliate you?" Mrs. Ripley wanted to know.

"By asking Mickey to sleep in the attic when you know perfectly well there are two beds in my room."

"It's not a question of the number of beds," Mr.
35 Ripley puffed. "There's a certain propriety about people sharing rooms when they're not married."

"What propriety?" Joan wanted to know.

Daughter's 'Friend' Is a Boy

by ART BUCHWALD

Mrs. Ripley said, "I know we're old-fashioned and out-of-date, but your father and I get very nervous
40 when we know two unmarried people of the opposite sex are in the same room under our roof."

"But Mickey and I aren't strangers," Joan protested. "Where do you think we live in Cambridge?"

"I don't want to know where you live in Cam-
45 bridge. You're not in Cambridge this weekend! You're in our house!" Mr. Ripley yelled.

"I thought it was my house, too," Joan said.

"It is your house, dear—but it's not Mickey's house. After all, it would seem to me you would
50 enjoy one weekend sleeping alone in your own room," Mrs. Ripley said.

"If I'd known this was going to be such a big deal," Joan said, "I wouldn't have come home."

"It's not a big deal," said Mr. Ripley. "It's a simple
55 question of moral standards. Ours seem to be different from yours. They may not be better but they are different."

"And that's why you want to ruin our weekend?" Joan asked.

60 "We're not trying to ruin your weekend, dear," Mrs. Ripley said. "What we're offering you are separate but equal accommodations. . . ."

"That's very funny," Joan said. "But all the way down in the car Mickey was counting on sleeping in
65 my room. He wouldn't have come if he had known he had to sleep in the attic."

Mr. Ripley said, "He'll sleep in your room over my dead body."

I decided to intercede. "I have a suggestion. Since
70 Mickey was counting on sleeping in Joan's room, why don't you let him sleep there and have Joan sleep in the attic?"

All three looked at me.

Then Mr. Ripley said, "Wait a minute. Suppose
75 Joan decides to come down from the attic in the middle of the night?"

"It's simple," I said. "Make Mickey promise to lock his door."

THE FAMILY CIRCUS   **by Bill Keane**

I HOPE THIS IS ONE OF THOSE GOOD OL' DAYS GRANDMA ALWAYS TALKS ABOUT.

3

The more difficult words in the selection you have just read are defined in the list below.* You may already know what some of the words mean; you may be able to guess the meanings of others from their **context** (what comes before and after a word); or you may want to refer to the list as you would a dictionary. Notice that in each word the <u>stressed</u> syllable is underlined; this will help you with your pronunciation of English words.

VOCABULARY LIST

tremendous *(adj.)*   very great; enormous

handle *(v.)*   to deal with (a problem or situation)

strapping *(adj.)*   tall, strong, healthy-looking

flustered *(adj.)*   nervous, confused

attic *(n.)*   space just below the roof in a house and above the other rooms

snarl *(v.)*   to growl angrily and show one's teeth (like a dog); speak angrily

humiliate *(v.)*   to shame; cause to feel ashamed

puff *(v.)*   to breathe quickly and hard

propriety *(n.)*   proper behavior

out-of-date *(adj.)*   old-fashioned

ruin *(v.)*   to spoil; destroy

accommodations *(n.)*   rooms (for rent) in a house, hotel, etc.

count on *(two-word verb)*   to express with certainty; depend on

intercede *(v.)*   to interfere in order to bring about an agreement between or among others

---

* Each of the first ten reading selections is followed by a vocabulary list; each word is defined and labeled a part of speech according to context.

Reading Comprehension

Answer the following statements True or False.

———————— 1. Mr. Buchwald implies (does not directly state) that Joan telephoned her parents to let them know she was bringing home a guest for the weekend.

———————— 2. Joan had been away at college.

———————— 3. Joan and Mickey had never shared a room.

———————— 4. The reader can conclude that there were two extra beds in the Ripley's house the weekend Joan and Mickey were there.

———————— 5. Mr. Ripley remained calm throughout the conversation with the two young people.

———————— 6. Mickey asked for some beer because he was thirsty after the long drive.

———————— 7. Joan couldn't understand her parents' point of view.

———————— 8. Mr. and Mrs. Ripley had the same standards of "right and wrong" as their daughter.

———————— 9. Mr. Buchwald decided to act as a peacemaker and suggested that Mickey sleep in the attic.

———————— 10. Mr. Buchwald's many readers find his columns amusing.

———————— 11. Art Buchwald's columns appear only in *The Atlanta Journal.*

QUESTIONS AND DISCUSSION

Answer the following questions.

1. Explain the expression "in the good old days." Why don't we say "in the *bad* old days"?
2. What is causing "tremendous houseguest problems throughout the country"?
3. Would these "problems" ever occur in your country? If so, how would the parents react?
4. How do you feel about a man and a woman living together before marriage?
5. Where do you think Art Buchwald got the idea for this column?
6. Do you think Art Buchwald approves of what Joan and Mickey are doing? Why do you think he is writing about it in a humorous manner?

Activity: Role Playing

Five students volunteer to act the part of the five persons in Mr. Buchwald's column. After studying the dialogue, the students stand in front of the class and read their respective parts.

Understanding Idioms

An *idiom* is an expression whose meaning cannot be understood from the meaning of each word in the expression. For example: "He's always in *hot water*" means "He's always in *trouble*." "He *kicked the bucket*" means "He *died*." Sometimes you can *guess* the meaning of an idiom from its *context*—what comes before and after the idiom.

MULTIPLE CHOICE

Read the following excerpts from the reading selection, and then choose the appropriate meaning for each of the <u>underlined</u> idioms.

_____ 1. " 'Why can't he sleep in my room?' Joan asked. Mr. Ripley <u>blew up</u>. 'Because I know he'd rather sleep in the attic.' " (lines 21–23)
   A. took a deep breath
   B. lost his temper
   C. made a loud noise

_____ 2. " 'There's a beer in the ice box. <u>Make yourself at home.</u>' " (line 27)
   A. Drink some beer.
   B. Don't leave the house.
   C. Relax and be comfortable.

_____ 3. " 'If I'd known this was going to be <u>such a big deal</u>,' Joan said, 'I wouldn't have come home.' " (lines 52–53)
   A. so immoral
   B. so impossible
   C. so important

Vocabulary

COMPOUND WORDS

A *compound* word is a combination of two or more words. For example: *house* + *guest* = *houseguest* (line 7). Consult your English-English dictionary to determine whether a compound word is written as one word (houseguest) or two words (alarm clock), or whether it is hyphenated (old-fashioned). The first part of a compound word is *usually* stressed.

*Each compound word below is a combination of **house** and another word. Fill in the blank in each of the following sentences with the appropriate compound word. The first one is done for you.*

housebound (adj.)   housekeeper   housewife
housecoat   housemate   housework

1. A mother who works outside the home needs a good ____*house-*____ ____*keeper*____.

2. After she took a shower, she put on her _____ and went into the kitchen to make breakfast.

3. In the good old days, a girl looked forward to becoming a _____ _____; now she looks forward to becoming a corporate executive.

4. Women nowadays expect their husbands to share in the _____ _____.

5. Jane's _____ paid half the rent and shared the other household expenses.

6. Because of the heavy snow, everyone was _____.

*Look through the reading selection and circle **all** the compound words.*

In English, a word can have more than one meaning; its use within a sentence determines whether it is a noun, verb, adjective, etc. For example, in line 11 of the reading selection, *handle* is a *verb* and means to *deal with* (a problem or situation); but in your English-English dictionary you will find that the *verb* handle has several other meanings. You will also find that *handle* can be a noun.

han·dle[1] /ˈhændl/ *n* **1** a part of an object which is especially made for holding it or for opening it—see illustration on page 95 **2** **fly off the handle** *infml* to lose one's temper

handle[2] *v* **-dled, -dling** [T] **1 a** to feel in the hands **b** to move by hand: *Glass—handle with care.* **2** to deal with; control: *He handled a difficult argument skillfully.* |*Ms. Brown handles the company's accounts.*|*A good teacher must know how to handle children.* **3** to use (goods) in business; DEAL in: *We don't handle that sort of book.*—**handleable** *adj.*

*Study the various meanings of **handle** in the dictionary entries listed to the left, and then complete the sentences below using the appropriate form of **handle** and any other words necessary to the meaning of the sentences. The first sentence is done as an example.*

1. That shop on the corner _____*handles newspapers and magazines*_____.

2. I can't open the car door because _____.

3. When you barbecue meat on an outdoor grill, you need a fork that has

    _____.

4. Don't _____ until you wash your hands.

5. I dropped the cup of coffee because _____.

6. Nurses who work in mental hospitals are trained to _____

    _____.

7. The woman's husband died, and with the help of her many friends, she

    _____ with courage.

8. A person can accidentally shoot himself if he doesn't know how to

    _____.

9. After Dan had forgotten to do his homework for five consecutive days,

    his teacher finally lost her patience and _____

    _____!

A **two-word** verb, also called *phrasal verb*, is a verb followed by a preposition or an adverb (particle) that changes the meaning of the verb. For example: the verb *count* has a different meaning when it is combined with *on*. *Count on* (line 70) means to *expect with certainty;* it can also mean to *depend on*.

There are a vast number of two-word verbs in the English language, but there are no rules for learning them. The more you read and listen to English, the easier it will be for you to recognize these verbs, to learn their meanings, and to use them correctly.

Study the two-word verbs and their definitions listed below, and then fill in each blank in the following sentences (page 10) with the appropriate two-word verb. Be sure to use the correct tense of the verb in each sentence.

count *(someone)* **in** *(S)**   to include (someone)

count *(someone)* **out** *(S)*   (1) to exclude (someone); (2) to declare (a fallen boxer) the loser when he cannot stand up after 10 seconds have been counted

count off *(S)*   to subtract, deduct

count on   to expect with certainty; to depend on

---

* (S) = *SEPARABLE:* A noun or pronoun object may separate (come between) the verb and the particle (preposition/adverb.)

    EXAMPLE: *Turn on* the TV.
             Turn the TV *on.*
             Turn it *on.*

    NOTE: A pronoun object *usually* comes between the verb and the particle.

    RIGHT: Turn *it* on.
    WRONG: Turn on *it.*

    INSEPARABLE: An inseparable two-word verb *cannot* have an object between the verb and the particle.

    EXAMPLE: Jane *counts on* her parents to send her money for tuition.
            Jane *counts on* them.

    NOTE: All intransitive two-word verbs (two-word verbs that do not take objects) are inseparable.

    EXAMPLE: I *got up* early this morning.
            Ali *gets along* well with all his classmates.

Whether a two-word verb is separable or inseparable must be memorized along with its meaning.

1. I _____ you to help me study for my exam.

2. I enjoy going to your parties; please _____ me _____ when you plan another!

3. My teacher always _____ two points for each mis-spelled word.

4. Angeline doesn't like to swim in the ocean, so her friends _____ her _____ when they go to the beach.

5. Martha _____ going* to the school dance with Antonio, but at the last minute he got sick.

6. The referee _____ the boxer _____ in the first round of the fight.

SYNONYMS

From the list below, choose the word or phrase that is closest in meaning to the underlined word or phrase in each of the following sentences. Write your answer in the blank after the sentence. Each of the ten words chosen should be used only once.

accommodations	flustered	propriety
attics	handle	ruin
count	humiliate	strapping
count on	out-of-date	tremendous

1. The president's wife would never wear an <u>old-fashioned</u> dress to a party in the White House. _____

2. Were you able to get good <u>rooms</u> at the Hilton? _____
   _____

3. He weighs over two hundred pounds because he has a <u>very big</u> appetite. _____

_____

* Notice that the -ing form of the verb is used after a two-word verb.

4. She became <u>nervous and confused</u> when she was unable to answer the teacher's question. _____

5. Football players are <u>strong and healthy</u> men. _____

6. A parent should never <u>shame</u> his child by spanking him in public. _____

7. I hope bad weather doesn't <u>spoil</u> our plans for a picnic. _____

8. <u>Proper behavior</u> demands that a man not go dancing soon after the death of his wife. _____

9. Thousands of senior citizens <u>depend on</u> their social security checks to buy the necessities of life. _____

10. Rita has learned to <u>manage</u> her job as an accountant efficiently. _____

President Jimmy Carter grew up on a farm near Plains, Georgia, a small town (population 683) in the southwestern part of the state. His father was a farmer and ran a farm products store.

President Carter was graduated from the United States Naval Academy in 1946. He served in the Navy until 1953, when, because of the death of his father, he returned to Plains to manage the family farm and peanut warehouse. From 1971 to 1975, he served as Governor of Georgia. In 1977, Mr. Carter became the thirty-ninth President of the United States. He remained president until 1981, when he was succeeded by Ronald Reagan, who had defeated him in the 1980 presidential election.

In the following excerpt from his autobiography, Why Not the Best?, *President Carter writes about his mother and father and remembers several incidents from his childhood.*

I never even considered disobeying my father, and he seldom if ever ordered me to perform a task; he simply suggested that it needed to be done, and he expected me to do it. But he was a stern disciplinarian and punished me severely when I misbehaved. From the time I was four years old until I was fifteen years old he whipped me six times and I've never forgotten any of those impressive experiences. The punishment was administered with a small, long, flexible peach tree switch.

My most vivid memory of a whipping was when I was four or five years old. I had been to my Sunday School class, and as was his custom Daddy had given me a penny for the offering. When we got home, I took off my Sunday clothes and put the contents of my pocket on a dresser. There were two pennies lying there. Daddy thus discovered that when they passed the collection plate I had taken out an extra penny, instead of putting mine in for the offering. That was the last money I ever stole.

Most of my other punishments occurred because of arguments with my sister Gloria, who was younger than I, but larger, during our growing years. I remember once she threw a wrench and hit me, and I retaliated by shooting her in the rear end with a B.B. gun. For several hours, she re-burst into tears every time the sound of a car was heard. When Daddy finally drove into our yard, she was apparently sobbing uncontrollably, and after a brief explanation by her of what had occurred, Daddy whipped me without further comment.

I never remember seeing Daddy without a hat on when he was outdoors. He laughed a lot and almost everybody liked him. He kept very thorough and

Why Not the Best?

by JIMMY CARTER

35 accurate farm and business records and was scrupulously fair with all those who dealt with him. He finished the tenth grade at Riverside Academy in Gainesville, Georgia, before the First World War. So far as I have been able to determine this was—at that
40 time—the most advanced education of any Carter since our family moved to Georgia more than 200 years ago.

My father died in July of 1953, a victim of cancer. He was extremely intelligent, well read about current
45 events, and was always probing for innovative business techniques or enterprises. He was quite conservative, and my mother* was and is a liberal, but within our family we never thought about trying to define such labels.

* Mrs. Lillian Carter died in 1983.

50 My mother is a registered nurse, and during my formative years she worked constantly, primarily on private duty either at the nearby hospital or in patients' homes. She typically worked on nursing duty twelve hours per day, or twenty hours per day for
55 which she was paid a magnificent six dollars, and during her off-duty hours she had to perform the normal functions of a mother and a housekeeper. She served as a community doctor for our neighbors and for us, and was extremely compassionate towards
60 all those who were afflicted with any sort of illness. Although my father seldom read a book, my mother was an avid reader, and so was I.

Quite often my mother was not paid for her nursing service at all, at least not in cash. I remember
65 once that for weeks Mother nursed a young girl who had diphtheria. The girl's parents were very poor. Eventually she died and a few weeks later the girl's father drove into our yard with a one-horse wagon loaded down with turpentine chips. He had traveled
70 more than a day to get there.

Although the wood chips had little monetary value, they were extremely helpful to us because they burst instantly into a roaring flame when touched with a match and were useful in starting a fire in the stove
75 or fireplace, an early morning necessity for us.** I remember that we unloaded the turpentine chips into a pit used for storing ferns and flowers during the winter, and we benefitted from their use for several years.

** The Carter farm had no electricity until 1937, when Jimmy Carter was 13 years old. The Rural Electrification Program was established by the federal government in 1935 to bring electricity to the rural areas of the United States.

Tools

Hammer   Pliers

Wrench   Screwdriver

excerpt *(n.)*   selected passage from a book, speech, etc.

task *(n.)*   work to be done; job

stern *(adj.)*   strict; demanding and enforcing obedience

flexible *(adj.)*   easily bent without breaking

vivid *(adj.)*   clear and distinct

offering *(n.)*   contribution given to a church

dresser *(n.)*   piece of furniture with drawers for clothes; bureau

wrench *(n.)*   tool to hold and turn nuts, bolts, etc.

retaliate *(v.)*   to return the same type of bad treatment that one has received

sob *(v.)*   to cry with short, quick breaths

fair *(adj.)*   just, honest

scrupulously *(adv.)* **fair**   being very careful to do nothing dishonest

probe *(v.)*   to investigate or examine thoroughly

innovative *(adj.)*   new (a new way of doing something)

conservative *(adj.)*   inclined to keep things as they are; opposed to change

liberal *(n.)*   a person who is in favor of change; an open-minded person

label *(n.)*   word or phrase used to describe some person, thing, or idea

formative *(adj.)*   pertaining to growth or development

compassionate *(adj.)*   wishing to help those who suffer; sympathetic

avid *(adj.)*   very interested; enthusiastic

chip *(n.)*   small piece (of wood, stone, etc.) separated by chopping, cutting, breaking

store *(v.)*   to put away for later use

Reading Comprehension

QUESTIONS AND DISCUSSION

Answer the following questions.

1. When was President Carter born? (Consult the second footnote on page 13.) Where did he spend most of his boyhood years? How long ago did his ancestors come to his native state? Did *you* grow up in a small town or a city? What are the advantages and disadvantages of living in a small town? A city?

2. How did Jimmy Carter's father earn a living? How much education did his father have? Would you conclude that President Carter's parents were poor? Explain your answer. Do you think President Carter admired and respected his parents? Give your reasons.

3. President Carter's mother was a nurse. Explain: "She served as a community doctor for our neighbors and us . . . ." Why do you think six dollars was considered a "magnificent sum" for a day's work? How much money do you think a registered nurse receives for eight hours' work today?

4. Why did Mrs. Carter value the turpentine chips she received as payment for her services? Why couldn't she afford an electric stove?

5. How did young Jimmy learn that "honesty is the best policy"? How do you think children should be disciplined? How were you disciplined when you were a child?

6. What high elective office did Jimmy Carter hold before 1977?

7. How many times did Jimmy Carter run for* President of the United States? How many times was he elected? Who succeeded him as President?

---

* *run for:* to be a candidate for

Idioms

The reading selection includes two idioms that contain the verb *burst* (lines 26 and 73):

burst into tears   to begin to cry suddenly

burst into flames   to burn suddenly and violently

Define the following two idioms without consulting your English-English dictionary.

burst into laughter _____

burst into bloom _____
    (*Hint:* What part of a plant is the bloom?)

Vocabulary

ORAL EXERCISE

Answer the following questions.

1. Tell about an incident in your childhood that made you *sob*.
2. A person should not choose certain occupations or professions if he or she is not *compassionate*. Explain.
3. Do you think *avid* readers usually make good students? Explain.
4. What household *tasks* do you think a man and his wife should share?
5. Do you think a mother should work outside the home during her child's *formative* years? State your reasons.
6. If you were writing an *autobiography*, what would you most likely say in the first chapter?
7. Whose *biography* would you like to read? Why?
8. Would reading an *excerpt* from a book encourage you to read the book or discourage you from reading it? Explain your answer.

PREFIXES

Part 1

A **prefix** is a syllable or syllables put at the beginning of a word to change the meaning of the word. A *negative* prefix gives a *negative* meaning to a word. *Dis-* (not); *mis-* (wrong; bad); and *un-* (not; opposite of) are a few of the many negative prefixes.

*Study the three examples in the following exercise. Form new words by adding the appropriate prefixes (**dis-, mis-,** or **un-**) to the words listed, and then write original sentences using each new word. Use your English-English dictionary to be sure of the correct meaning of each new word.*

Dis-

Example: obey (v.)   __*disobey*__ (line 1)

1. _____

     _____

       agree (v.)   _____

2. _____

     _____

       honest (adj.)   _____

3. _____

     _____

       courteous (adj.)   _____

4. _____

     _____

Example: behave (*v.*) <u>*misbehave* (line 5)</u>

5. _____

_____

pronounce (*v.*) _____

6. _____

_____

spell (*v.*) _____

7. _____

_____

understand (*v.*) _____

8. _____

_____

Un-

Example: load (*v.*) <u>*unload* (line 76)</u>

9. _____

happy (*adj.*) _____

10. _____

able (*adj.*) _____

11. _____

lock (*v.*) _____

12. _____

Part 2

Some other common negative prefixes are *in-, im-, il-, ir-* **(not)**; and *non-* **(not)**, *anti-* **(against)**, and *mal-* **(bad)**.

Underline the **prefix** in each of the words listed below, and then fill in each blank in the following sentences with the appropriate word from the list. Use your English-English dictionary if necessary.

antisocial	impossible	irrelevant
illegible	inhumane	malnutrition
illiterate	inseparable	nonviolence
impatiently	irregular	nonsmokers

1. It was _____ to correct the student's test paper because his handwriting was _____.

2. Our professor cautioned us that _____ class attendance would affect our final grade for the course.

3. Children whose parents cannot afford to feed them properly often suffer from _____.

4. An _____ two-word verb cannot have an object between the verb and the particle.

5. _____ persons miss the pleasure of reading.

6. Martin Luther King believed in _____ to bring about social and economic reforms for black people.

7. In the cafeteria at Georgia State University, there are several tables reserved for _____.

8. She waited _____ in line to use the public telephone.

9. All George's comments were _____ to the subject we were discussing.

10. Because he was too shy to talk to his classmates, they thought he was _____.

11. Society abhors the _____ treatment of animals.

Note: There are no rules to help you determine which negative prefix to use before a particular word; use your English-English dictionary if you are uncertain.

Part 3

Choose the best answer for each of the following statements.

_____ 1. After the party was over, the hostess noticed quite a lot of uneaten food on the plates.
A. There was not enough food for the guests.
B. The food was not very good.
C. There was no food left.
D. The guests "cleaned" their plates.

_____ 2. It's illegal to park in a space reserved for the handicapped.
A. The law states that handicapped people can't drive.
B. Only the handicapped can lawfully park in certain spaces.
C. Lawyers help handicapped people find parking spaces.
D. Handicapped people are not able to park their cars.

_____ 3. His unscheduled arrival interfered with my plans.
A. He wrote me his flight schedule.
B. My schedule was flexible.
C. I was surprised by his visit.
D. He scheduled his visit after he arrived.

_____ 4. It was unusual for Juan to be absent, so his teacher assumed he had misread the bus schedule.
A. Juan's teacher assumed Juan had forgotten to read the bus schedule.
B. Juan's teacher thought Juan had missed the bus as usual.
C. Juan's teacher assumed Juan had not read the bus schedule correctly.
D. Juan's teacher assumed that Juan didn't want to come to class.

_____ 5. She is a nonstop talker.
A. She is very shy.
B. She never stops to talk to her friends.
C. She stops talking when others interrupt.
D. She loves to talk.

You have learned that a word can have more than one meaning; its use within a sentence determines whether it is a noun, verb, adjective, etc. (page 8).

Part 1

Some words that appear in the reading selection at the beginning of the chapter have more than one meaning:

flexible (line 9)   *conservative* (line 46)
switch (line 10)   *label* (line 49)
vivid (line 11)   *chip* (line 69)
dresser (line 16)   *store* (line 77)
fair (line 36)

Fill in each blank in the following sentences with the appropriate word from the list above. Each word will be used more than once. Label each word the appropriate part of speech. Use your English-English dictionary when necessary. Use correct verb tenses. The first sentence is done as an example.

1. The comb and brush are on the _____ *N.* _____ *dresser* _____.

2. Since my schedule is _____, I can see you in my office at any time.

3. I was afraid I would _____ my tooth on the small bones that were in the beef stew.

4. _____ meat in the freezer so that it won't spoil.

5. Rubber is a _____ material.

6. One does not have to buy expensive clothes to be a good _____.

7. The old lady has many _____ memories of her youth.

8. She has blond hair and a _____ complexion.

9. A _____ person does not favor change and new ideas.

10. My teacher told me that my term paper was not good, just _____.

11. You can't _____ that man a liberal; his ideas are too conservative.

12. He wanted to be a newspaper reporter, so he _____ his major from philosophy to journalism.

13. The weatherman predicted _____ weather for tomorrow.

14. Red and orange are _____ colors.

15. I'm looking for a _____ that sells health foods.

16. The _____ on the bottle identified its poisonous contents.

17. The father was not _____ because he punished one son when both sons misbehaved.

18. President Carter remembers being punished with a _____ from a peach tree.

19. Businesspeople should wear _____ clothes to the office—not blue jeans.

20. A _____ of wood flew into his eye while he was cutting down the tree.

Part 2

*Find the sentences in Part 1 (pages 21–22) that contain each of the following words. Put the number of each sentence in the appropriate blank. Then give a **definition** for each of the words listed according to its meaning in the sentence. Do not use your dictionary. Follow the example.*

_1_	dresser	*a piece of furniture with drawers for clothes*
_6_	dresser	*one who wears clothes in a specified way*
____	flexible	_____
____	flexible	_____
____	chip	_____
____	chip	_____

_____ store _____

_____ store _____

_____ vivid _____

_____ vivid _____

_____ fair _____

_____ fair _____

_____ fair _____

_____ fair _____

_____ conservative _____

_____ conservative _____

_____ label _____

_____ label _____

_____ switch _____

_____ switch _____

WORD GROUPS

Circle the one word that does not belong with the other four and explain why.

1. switch (v.)
   hit
   fight
   spank
   beat

2. peanuts
   cattle
   corn
   beans
   peaches

3. dresser
   table
   stove
   bed
   chair

4. wagon
   automobile
   bus
   bicycle
   boat

5. wrench
   hammer
   pliers
   nail
   screwdriver

6. diphtheria
   influenza
   cancer
   measles
   pneumonia

Lewis Grizzard writes a 4-day-a-week col-umn for The Atlanta Constitution *and* The Atlanta Journal *and is syndicated nationally. He is known as a humorist, but he also writes of serious matters. In "They Mourned Steve Vann in Silence," he tells the true story of a boy who dies needlessly and tragically.*

On a cloudy day, spring's first rain approaching, they came by the hundreds to mourn the death of Steve Vann. One of the preachers got up and said, "This is the Christian act of mourning. That is why
5 we are here."

The chapel was packed with people who had known him, who had loved him. Who still did. Per-haps now more than ever. The hallways outside the chapel were also crowded. Those who couldn't find
10 standing room inside waited in silence outside. Grief is rarely loud.

He was 17. He was a senior at Lakeside High School in DeKalb County. He was a quarterback on the football team. He lived in an upper middle-class
15 neighborhood. He had a lot of friends. He had par-ents who gave him their time and their attention and, of course, their love.

Saturday morning, somebody found him dead in a creek.
20 "There were all sorts of rumors going around," said a classmate at the funeral. "Somebody at first said he had been stabbed. I knew that wasn't true. If Steve had an enemy, I never heard about it."

The county coroner was on television trying to
25 explain it. Steve Vann died of exposure to cold. He was found in creek water that had been below freez-ing the night before. The temperatures the night before were also below freezing.

Evidence of drugs was found in Steve Vann's body.
30 There was no overdose, but there were drugs.

I talked to more classmates at the funeral.

"I don't guess anybody will really ever know what happened," said one. "He went to a party Friday night, but Steve just wasn't the type to take anything.

They Mourned Steve Vann in Silence

by LEWIS GRIZZARD

terback, but Lakeside is a state power with a huge student body from which to draw its talent.

55 "He had the best arm on the team," somebody said. "It hurt him that he wasn't a starter, but he threw a touchdown pass in one of the last games. He must have thrown the ball 60 yards."

But it happened. Steve Vann's death was drug-related. There is no way to hide it.

60 A young man standing outside the chapel said, between puffs on a cigarette, "If this don't make you think, nothing will."

I could make this a sermon. Parents tell your children. Teachers shout it. Drugs kill. What I had 65 rather do is take you back to the funeral. There can be no more drastic lesson.

There were flowers, always there are flowers, and their scent inside a funeral home is a sickening sweet.

The casket was a metallic blue. There were flowers 70 on top of it. The mother cried hard. The father looked stunned. Old people hung their heads. Young people stared in disbelief.

An organ played softly. A man sang, "Will the Circle Be Unbroken?" and "I Come to the Garden 75 Alone" and "The Lord's Prayer."

One preacher said, "We are all in shock."

Another said, "This is a great tragedy."

A third said, "He esteemed his elders, he respected his leaders, he was growing into a man of worth."

80 And at the end, the father walked to the podium and spoke from his breaking heart.

"If any of you are ever in trouble," he told his son's friends, "if any of you need any help, or need to talk, then come to me. This," he went on, looking 85 at the casket before him, "is enough."

God bless him for saying that.

35 He might have smoked some grass, most everybody else does; but I can't see him drinking and taking pills."

"Somebody could have slipped him something," added another. "I knew him as well as anybody in 40 school, and he knew better."

The death has been ruled an accident. The most popular conjecture is Steve Vann, because of the drugs, became disoriented, wandered into the creek and remained there—unconscious—until the cold 45 killed him.

Something like this shouldn't happen here, I was telling myself at the funeral. Look around you, I said. This isn't the ghetto. This is suburbia, good life America.

50 Steve Vann was no mindless punk.

He was an athlete. He was the second-string quar-

mourn *(v.)* to feel or show sorrow

grief *(n.)* deep sorrow or sadness

creek *(n.)* small river

sorts *(n.)* kinds

rumor *(n.)* story or statement that is not known to be true; gossip

funeral *(n.)* ceremonies performed when a dead person's body is buried or burned (cremated)

stab *(v.)* to stick a knife or sharp-pointed weapon into somebody

coroner *(n.)* an official who investigates any death that appears not to be from natural causes

evidence *(n.)* whatever proves or disproves something

grass *(n.) (slang)* marijuana

conjecture *(n.)* guess; formation of an opinion without sufficient evidence for proof

disoriented *(adj.)* confused (not knowing where one is)

wander *(v.)* to go from place to place because of confusion; go from place to place without any special purpose

ghetto *(n.)* section of a city lived in by very poor people, usually a minority group

punk *(n.) (slang)* worthless person

stunned *(adj.)* shocked; dazed (as from some very bad news)

tragedy *(n.)* very sad event

esteem *(v.)* to have a very favorable opinion of; respect

podium *(n.)* platform (for a conductor of an orchestra or a lecturer, etc.)

Reading Comprehension

QUESTIONS AND DISCUSSION

Answer the following questions.

1. What is a funeral?
2. Why does Lewis Grizzard use each of the following words in his description of Steve Vann's funeral?

   mourn (line 2)   *grief* (line 10)
   preacher (line 3)   *flowers* (line 67)
   chapel (line 6)   *casket* (line 69)

3. Does every religion have its own special ceremonies for the burial or cremation of the dead? If someone of your own faith dies, what kind of funeral does he/she have? Is cremation permitted?
4. What do most people think happened to Steve Vann from the time he left a party one Friday night until he was discovered dead in a creek the following morning? What was one of the early rumors about the cause of his death?
5. What is a coroner and what does he do? (Look up the word *autopsy* in your English-English dictionary.) Was Steve Vann's death drug-related? Explain.
6. Does Lewis Grizzard imply (suggest) that Steve Vann had a good and happy life? Explain.
7. What does Mr. Grizzard mean when he writes, "What I had rather do is take you back to the funeral. There can be no more drastic lesson."
8. How did Steve's father offer to help his son's friends who might be in trouble?
9. Do you think Steve Vann knowingly took drugs the night he died? Why do you think so many young people take drugs? Is there drug abuse in your country, and if so, what is being done to combat it?

MULTIPLE CHOICE

Choose the correct answer.

_____ 1. Before Steve Vann's death, he
   A. was failing all his courses at Lakeside High.
   B. was in his last year at Lakeside High.
   C. had been arrested for smoking grass.

_____ 2. The coroner investigated the cause of Steve's death because
A. Steve appeared not to have died from natural causes.
B. he knew Steve had taken drugs.
C. Steve became disoriented.

_____ 3. The coroner concluded that Steve Vann's death was
A. a murder.
B. an accident.
C. a suicide.

_____ 4. Steve Vann died from
A. an overdose of drugs.
B. drowning.
C. exposure to freezing weather.

_____ 5. Steve lived with his family
A. in a ghetto.
B. in the suburbs.
C. in a mansion.

_____ 6. The words _quarterback_ and _touchdown_ refer to which one of the following sports:
A. baseball
B. basketball
C. football

_____ 7. Steve Vann
A. was very popular.
B. had few friends.
C. did not get along with his parents.

Meaning from Context

MULTIPLE CHOICE

Read the following excerpts from the reading selection. Choose the appropriate **meaning** for each underlined part of the sentences. Use the **context**—what comes before and after a word, phrase, sentence, etc.—to help you choose the correct meaning.

_____ 1. "The chapel was packed with people .... The hallways outside the chapel were also crowded. <u>Those who couldn't find standing room inside</u> waited in silence outside." (lines 6–10)
A. All the people inside the chapel were seated.
B. Everyone inside the chapel had to stand.
C. All the seats were taken and there was no more space to stand inside the chapel.

_____ 2. "'He went to a party Friday night, but Steve just wasn't the type to take anything ....'"
"'<u>Somebody could have slipped him something</u>,' added another." (lines 33–39)
A. He could have taken some drugs unknowingly.
B. He could have slipped into the creek.
C. Someone could have forced him to take drugs.

_____ 3. "'<u>He had the best arm on the team</u>,' somebody said .... 'he threw a touchdown pass in one of the last games. He must have thrown the ball 60 yards.'" (lines 54–57)
A. His arm was strong enough to throw the ball.
B. Only one of his arms was strong.
C. He could throw the ball long and accurately.

_____ 4. "And at the end, <u>the father</u> walked to the podium and <u>spoke from his breaking heart</u>." (lines 80–81)
A. Steve's father was very sad.
B. Steve's father almost had a heart attack.
C. Steve's father spoke about his weak heart.

| **WHAT DO YOU THINK?** | *Below are three excerpts from the selection. What do you think the <u>underlined</u> portion of each excerpt means? Pay attention to the* **context.** |

1. "Those who couldn't find standing room inside waited in silence outside. <u>Grief is rarely loud.</u>" (lines 9–11)
2. "This isn't the ghetto. <u>This is suburbia, good life America.</u>" (lines 48–49)
3. "There were flowers, always there are flowers, and <u>their scent inside a funeral home is a sickening sweet.</u>" (lines 67–68)
(*Hint:* In the United States, there are many flowers at a funeral, especially if the deceased had a lot of friends.)

Vocabulary

WORD GROUPS

Circle the one word that does not belong in some way with the other three and explain why.

1. football, soccer, swimming, tennis
2. creek, lake, river, island
3. chapel, church, theater, mosque
4. suburbia, poverty, ghetto, hunger
5. casket, wedding, funeral, graduation
6. senior, student, teacher, freshman
7. grass, pot, cigarette, punk
8. Christian, Islam, Moslem, Jew

ANTONYMS

An **antonym** is a word that is opposite in meaning to another. For example: *fast* is the antonym of *slow*.

You have already learned the meaning of each word in column (1) below. Choose the correct antonym in column (2) for each word in column (1). Use your English-English dictionary when necessary.

	(1)	**(2)**
_____	1. tremendous	A. fat
_____	2. strapping	B. modern
_____	3. out-of-date	C. dull
_____	4. stern	D. joy
_____	5. flexible	E. weak
_____	6. vivid	F. stiff
_____	7. conservative	G. tiny
_____	8. compassionate	H. cruel
_____	9. slender	I. liberal
_____	10. grief	J. lenient

TWO-WORD VERBS

A **two-word verb** or **phrasal verb** is a verb followed by a preposition or adverb (particle) that changes the meaning of the verb (page 9). For example: the verb *get* has a different meaning when it is combined with *up*. *Get up* (see line 3 of the reading) means to *rise from a chair or stand up*. It also means to *awake*.

Study the two-word verbs and their definitions listed below, and then fill in each blank in the following sentences with the appropriate two-word verb (and preposition, if necessary). Use the correct tense of the verb in each sentence.

get along *(with)*   to be friendly

get away *(from)*   (1) to escape; (2) to leave

get back *(from)*   to return

get off   (1) to leave (a bus, train, etc.); (2) to end work

get on   to enter (a bus, train, etc.)

get out *(of)*   (1) to leave; (2) to be dismissed or released

get out of*   to free oneself from an obligation

get over   to recover from (an illness or disappointment)

get through *(with)*   to finish

get to   to arrive at

get up   (1) to rise from a chair or stand up; (2) to awake

1. It usually takes a few days to _____ a cold.
2. I ran after the man who stole my purse, but he _____.
3. The young man _____ and offered the old lady his seat.
4. Nancy _____ all her classmates.
5. After she said good-bye to her boyfriend, she _____ the plane that would take her a thousand miles away.
6. Let's plan to go skating tomorrow. What time do you _____ _____ school?
7. When did you _____ your vacation?
8. After he bought an alarm clock, he was able to _____ on time.
9. Alex _____ work at eight o'clock every morning and _____ at four every afternoon.

---

* three-word verb

10. _____ that vicious dog before he bites you!

11. Billy parked his car and _____ to see if he had a flat tire.

12. When you _____ that book, may I borrow it?

13. I promised Jane I would go to a movie with her tonight. Now I don't want to go, but I can't _____ it.

14. Tommy didn't _____ the bus on Decatur Street because he had fallen asleep in his seat.

CHOOSING PARTICLES

Fill in each blank in the following paragraph with the appropriate particle* from the list below. You will not use all the particles in the list, and two particles will be used twice.

across	*in*	*over*
along	*off*	*up*
away	*on*	
down	*out*	

Juan didn't get _____ with his English teacher. He almost blew _____ when he found out she had counted _____ ten points for a misspelled word on his test. He was seated at his desk, but he got _____ and walked to the front of the classroom so that he could speak with her privately. He asked if he could see her in her office after he got _____ of his 12:45 class. She said, "I'll be glad to talk to you now. I know you're angry with me, but I hope you'll get _____ it. I realize you're working your way through school, and it's hard to study at night after you get _____ work. You should try to get _____ on the week-ends and relax. I do want you to know you can count _____ me to be fair."

---

* The preposition/adverb part of a two-word verb will now be called simply a *particle*.

Choose the word or phrase that is closest in meaning to the <u>underlined</u> word or phrase in the sentence.

_____ 1. A person who has a high fever sometimes becomes <u>confused</u>.
A. unconscious   C. nervous
B. disoriented   D. upset

_____ 2. I have all <u>sorts</u> of flowers growing in my garden.
A. scents   C. sizes
B. colors   D. kinds

_____ 3. Even though he didn't cry, one could see the <u>grief</u> on his face.
A. anger   C. tears
B. deep sadness   D. fear

_____ 4. Children should <u>esteem</u> their parents.
A. support   C. love
B. follow   D. respect

_____ 5. The <u>gossip</u> was that he was going to divorce his wife.
A. truth   C. fact
B. rumor   D. proof

_____ 6. People throughout the world <u>mourned</u> the death of President John Kennedy.
A. felt sorrow over C. were angry about
B. were shocked by D. spoke about

_____ 7. The thug robbed the man and then <u>stuck a knife into</u> him.
A. shot   C. choked
B. killed   D. stabbed

_____ 8. The flowers in the vase have a lovely <u>smell</u>.
A. bloom   C. cent
B. scent   D. color

_____ 9. The <u>conjecture</u> was that the airplane had crashed because of ice on the wings.
A. guess   C. truth
B. evidence   D. conclusion

_____ 10. The death of a child is a <u>very sad event</u>.
A. travesty   C. funeral
B. ceremony   D. tragedy

John F. Kennedy, at 43 years of age, was the youngest man ever elected President of the United States. In 1961, he became the thirty-fifth president, succeeding Dwight Eisenhower.

President Kennedy was born in Brookline, Massachusetts, a suburb of Boston. His father, Joseph P. Kennedy, was a self-made millionaire, who gave ten million dollars to each of his nine children. He sent his second son, John, to Harvard University, from where he was graduated in 1940.

During World War II, John Kennedy served in the South Pacific. He was twice decorated by the Navy for his heroism and leadership.

After the war, he decided to enter politics. In 1946, he was elected to the United States House of Representatives. He remained a congressman until 1952, when he was elected to the Senate.

On November 22, 1963, President Kennedy traveled to Texas to campaign for a second term as president. While riding in a motorcade to a luncheon in Dallas, he was shot and killed by a sniper hidden on the second floor of a school book depository.

The following is an excerpt from Kennedy, *a biography, written by Theodore C. Sorensen, who was special counsel to President Kennedy.*

President Kennedy's day at the White House did not begin at any heroic predawn hour. Awakening around 7:30 A.M., he quickly read the morning papers and often placed calls on their contents. Throughout
5 the day and night, as more newspapers and reports came in, more Presidential phone calls or terse memoranda would follow, inquiring, requesting, suggesting. Action was always expected as soon as possible. He was on the telephone, according to one estimate,
10 more than fifty times in an average day, with a large portion of the calls taking place in the Mansion before and after his hours in the office.

After a bath, shaving as always in the tub to save time, breakfast was around 8:45—sometimes with his
15 family if they were available, sometimes in bed with the newspapers, and once or twice a week on official business, with legislative leaders, staff members or others.

Between 9:00 and 9:30 A.M. he arrived in his office,
20 checked his mail, read a three-thousand-word CIA briefing and plunged into the day's round of conferences. In addition to the official calendar of appoint-

Kennedy

by THEODORE SORENSEN

40 larger picture. When he considered a subject ex-
hausted or a decision final, he would gather up all
his papers as a sign that the meeting was over and,
if this hint was not taken by persistent conferees,
suddenly rise to his feet to say good-bye.

45 . . . the president was often an hour behind schedule by the end of his day. It was always an exhaust-
ingly full and long day, as he remained in the office
until 7:30, 8:00 or even 8:30 P.M., sometimes return-
ing after his customarily late dinner, and usually
50 reading reports and memoranda in the Mansion until
midnight. Even when he had guests for dinner and
a movie, he would often slip away after fifteen minutes of the film to work, and then rejoin them when
it was over. More than once we worked in his West
55 Wing oval office or in his bedroom or oval study in
the Mansion until well past midnight. More than
once after a late dinner I would invite guests to view
the Presidential office only to find him there going
over mail or other documents. Saturdays, when he
60 was in Washington, were usually a shorter working
day, and on Sundays no regular office hours were
kept. But it all added up to an average of forty-five
to fifty-five hours of work weekly in his office and
still more over in the Mansion. "He lived at such a
65 pace," his wife has said, "because he wished to know
it all."

He helped himself maintain such a pace by wisely
breaking his day for two hours or so at lunch.
Around 1:30, and if possible, a second time in the
70 evening, he would take a fifteen-minute swim in the
heated (90-degree) White House pool, usually with
Dave Powers.* Even at the height of the Cuban crisis** he made time for his dip in the pool. Listening
to recorded show music in the background, exchang-
75 ing sports stories or anecdotes with Powers, he re-
generated his energies and ideas, often giving Dave a
list of messages he wanted delivered during the lunch

---

* *Dave Powers:* one of President Kennedy's aides
** *Cuban crisis:* The United States demanded that
Russia remove its missiles from Cuban soil.

---

ments released to the press, he had a far larger number of off-the-record meetings and a still larger
25 number of informal talks with staff aides. Daily
events often required new meetings to be squeezed
into the schedule . . . .

He kept meetings as brief as the subject permitted,
many no more than fifteen minutes, very few running
30 over an hour, but when necessary sitting for several
hours. For long afternoon meetings, he often ordered
coffee served to all hands. He kept his own comments
to a minimum and often cut short others, no matter
how important or friendly, who were dealing with
35 generalities or repeating the obvious. Frequently he
saw their point long before they had finished. Focusing full attention upon each speaker, even while
doodling on a pad before him, he had a remarkable
ability to absorb detail while keeping in view the

hour. The swim, a rubdown and his calisthenics were followed by lunch—occasionally official affairs with foreign dignitaries, editors, or business or labor leaders, but more often private. He continued to read while lunching if he were alone—and then he would read or nap in bed while easing his back on a hotpad. Between three and four o'clock he was back in his office or on his way to a press conference, refreshed and ready to act . . . .

In a larger sense, the President's office is wherever the President may be. For unlike the Congress and Supreme Court, the Presidency never recesses or adjourns. Unlike the arrangement in most departments and states, his absence from the country does not make his running mate Acting President. Wherever he went, Kennedy was linked by telephone to the White House switchboard, guarded by the Secret Service, and discreetly followed by one of an alternating team of Army warrant officers carrying in a slender black case the secret codes by which the Presidential order for nuclear retaliation would be given. Wherever he went, he received the same daily CIA briefing from a military or other aide and read most of the same daily newspapers, which were flown in to him if necessary. Wherever he went, he took with him the bulky black alligator briefcase he had carried since his first days in the House—the same bag he often took over to the Mansion in the evening—bulging with whatever he and his staff felt he needed to read by way of mail, magazines, books, briefing memos and assorted dispatches and documents. During absences of forty-eight hours or more, additional materials were flown to him regularly. Wherever he went, he kept in constant touch with Washington, signed bills and Executive Orders, and conferred on or contemplated current crises.

VOCABULARY LIST

terse *(adj.)*   brief and to the point; short

memorandum *(n.)*, **memoranda** *(pl.)*   informal message, especially one sent between offices

Mansion *(n.)*   Executive Mansion or White House

CIA   Central Intelligence Agency (of the U.S. government)

briefing *(n.)*   act of giving concise information, instructions, or advice

plunge *(v.)*   to enter suddenly into an activity

press *(n.)*   newspapers and magazines and those who write for them

aide *(n.)*   assistant

focus *(v.)*   to concentrate

doodle *(v.)*   to make drawings or scribble absentmindedly while talking or thinking

hint *(n.)*   small and indirect suggestion

pace *(n.)*   rate; speed

crisis *(n.)*, **crises** *(pl.)*   deciding event in history; time of danger and anxious waiting

anecdote *(n.)*   short story concerning an interesting event

rubdown *(n.)*   massage

nap *(v.)*   to sleep for a short time, often during the day

ease *(v.)*   to lessen the pain of

recess *(v.)*   to take a recess

recess or **recess** *(n.)*   time during which work stops

adjourn *(v.)*   to bring (a meeting, trial, etc.) to an end until a later time or indefinitely

slender *(adj.)*   slim; not wide

bulky *(adj.)*   large

dispatch *(n.)*   written message, such as special news or government business

Reading Comprehension

WRITTEN EXERCISE

Answer the following questions.

1. Which of the following statements about President Kennedy and President Carter are true? Put a check (√) in front of each true statement.

_____ a. They were both from the South.

_____ b. Both of their fathers were millionaires.

_____ c. They were both in the United States Navy.

_____ d. They both served in the United States Congress before they became President.

_____ e. They both lived in the Mansion.

_____ f. Neither served more than one term as President.

_____ g. They were both avid readers.

2. How does the reader know that President Kennedy was not a time-waster? Give several examples.

_____

_____

_____

3. Name three ways President Kennedy liked to relax.

_____

_____

_____

4. The President's office is "wherever the President may be." Explain.

_____

_____

_____

5. Approximately how long was John F. Kennedy President of the United States?

_____

TRUE/FALSE STATEMENTS

Answer the following statements True or False. *Explain why the statements are true or false in the spaces provided.*

_____ 1. The reader can infer (conclude) that the Presidents of the United States can leave home and arrive at their office in a matter of minutes.

_____

_____ 2. President Kennedy, like many of his countrymen, worked an eight-hour day.

_____

_____ 3. The reader can conclude that President Kennedy thought the telephone was a poor means of communication.

_____

_____ 4. According to the excerpt, the President's schedule was inflexible.

_____

_____ 5. Even during a time of great danger to his country, the President took time to exercise.

_____

_____ 6. The reader can infer that President Kennedy suffered from backaches.

_____

_____ 7. The Vice-President takes the place of the President when the latter is out of the country.

_____

Meaning from Context

MULTIPLE CHOICE

Read the following excerpts from the reading selection. Choose the appropriate **meaning** for each of the underlined expressions. Pay close attention to the **context**.

_____ 1. "In addition to the official calendar of appointments released to the press, he had a far larger number of <u>off-the-record</u> meetings . . . ." (lines 22–24)
A. official
B. rehearsed
C. (meetings that were) not for publication

_____ 2. "Even when he had guests for dinner and a movie, he would often <u>slip away</u> after fifteen minutes of the film to work, and then rejoin them when it was over." (lines 51–54)
A. leave unnoticed
B. whisper good-bye
C. take a nap

_____ 3. "For unlike the Congress and Supreme Court, The Presidency never recesses or adjourns . . . . his [the President's] absence from the country does not make his <u>running mate</u> Acting President." (lines 88–92)
A. wife
B. Secretary of State
C. Vice-President

_____ 4. "Wherever he went, he <u>kept in</u> constant <u>touch with</u> Washington . . . ." (lines 110–111)
A. made speeches about
B. communicated with
C. thought about

| **WHAT DO YOU THINK?** | *What do you think the following excerpts mean?* |

1. "Focusing full attention upon each speaker, . . . he had a remarkable ability to absorb detail while keeping in view the larger picture." (lines 36–40)
(*Hint:* Does the "larger picture" consist of details?)
2. "Wherever he went, Kennedy was . . . discreetly followed by one of an alternating team of Army warrant officers carrying in a slender black case the secret codes by which the Presidential order for nuclear retaliation would be given." (lines 92–98)
(*Hint:* What happens if there is a nuclear attack on the United States while the President is traveling?)

Vocabulary

PREFIXES

You have learned that a prefix changes the meaning of a word (page 17). Two frequently used prefixes are *pre-* (before) and *re-* (again; back). For example: *pre* + dawn = *predawn* or before dawn (line 2); *re* + join = *rejoin* or join again (line 53).

Part 1

Rewrite the following sentences, substituting the appropriate meaning for each of the underlined words. (If necessary, change the word order of the sentence to make the definition fit into the context.)

1. I can't <u>recall</u>* the name of that good movie I saw on television last week.

   _____

   _____

2. Always <u>review</u> your notes before you take a test.

   _____

   _____

3. The plane stopped in Atlanta to <u>refuel</u>.

   _____

   _____

4. I like the magazine so I'm going to <u>renew</u> my subscription for another year.

   _____

   _____

5. Joan's parents did not approve of <u>premarital</u> sex.

   _____

   _____

---

* Some words prefixed by *re-* and *pre-* have special meanings; consult your English-English dictionary.

6. A driver's license is a <u>prerequisite</u> for being allowed to drive in the State of Georgia.

_____

_____

7. Nurseries provide day care for <u>preschool</u> children.

_____

_____

8. The dinosaur is a <u>prehistoric</u> animal.

_____

_____

Note: The prefix *post-* means *after*. Define the <u>underlined</u> words in the following sentences.

1. The European nations suffered <u>postwar</u> problems.
2. Don't cash my check today; I'm <u>postdating</u> it.

Part 2

Choose the best answer.

_____ 1. He is in prison for life because *his crime was premeditated.*
  A. He committed a crime in self-defense.
  B. He was so angry he committed a crime without thinking.
  C. He planned the crime he committed.
  D. He committed a crime before he went to prison.

_____ 2. Mary rejoined the French club.
  A. Mary resigned from the French club.
  B. Mary organized a new French club.
  C. Mary enjoyed being a member of the French club.
  D. Mary was bored with the French club.

_____ 3. Her baby was premature.
  A. Her baby was not very smart.
  B. Her baby was born in eight months.
  C. Her baby was very large.
  D. Her baby was born late.

_____ 4. The antique table that was destroyed in the fire can never be replaced.
   A. There is no other table like the one that was destroyed in the fire.
   B. There is no place to put another antique table.
   C. The fire destroyed everything in the place.
   D. Antique tables are difficult to find.

_____ 5. Lend me ten dollars and *I'll repay you next month*.
   A. I'll pay you again next month.
   B. I'll pay you back next month.
   C. I'll pay you in advance next month.
   D. I'll give you back pay next month.

TWO-WORD VERBS

A **two-word verb** is a verb followed by a particle that changes the meaning of the verb (page 9). Two-word verbs are also called *phrasal verbs* and *idioms*.

The two-word verbs listed below are combinations of the verb **run** *and a particular particle. Study them and their definitions and then fill in each blank in the following sentences with the appropriate two-word verb (and preposition, if necessary). Use the correct tense of the verb in each sentence.*

run across   to find unexpectedly; to meet by chance

run away *(from)*   to leave, escape

run down   to stop working (clocks, batteries, etc.)

run into   (1) to crash into; (2) to meet by chance

run out *(of)*   to use up, to have none left

run over   (1) to drive over, usually accidentally; (2) to overflow; (3) to go beyond (an hour, etc.) (line 29)

run up *(S)*   to increase (bills or debts)

1. I accidentally _____ the bicycle which was lying in the driveway.

2. I _____ an old friend yesterday; we were so happy to see each other.

3. You can't start your car because the battery has _____.

4. I _____ a big bill at the department store last Christmas.

5. When he _____ money, he calls up his father.

6. Some people _____ their problems by getting drunk.

7. I _____ an article in the newspaper that I think you would enjoy reading.

8. A drunk driver _____ my car yesterday.

RUN + PARTICLE

Fill in each of the blanks in the following story with the appropriate particle from the list below. <u>One</u> of the particles will <u>not</u> be used.

away	*in*	*over*
across	*into*	*up*
down	*out*	

Margie was baking a birthday cake for her little daughter when she ran _____ of butter. She hurried to the grocery store. While she was standing in the checkout line, she ran _____ Raffaella.

"Hi, Raffaella. I'm giving a birthday party for my daughter. I ran _____ a good recipe in yesterday's paper, and I decided to bake a cake."

"I went shopping for clothes today," Raffaella answered. "My husband wishes my car battery would run _____ so that I wouldn't run _____ such big bills!"

"Well, I have to hurry home to finish the cake. I hope I don't have a flat tire. I think I ran _____ a nail on the way here."

"Margie, I hope your little girl has a nice birthday. I feel like running _____ sometimes; you know, nine kids can run you up the wall!"*

---

* *run you up the wall*: drive you crazy

Fill in the blanks in the following sentences with the appropriate words from the list below. The <u>ten</u> words chosen should be used only <u>once</u>. Use correct verb tenses.

adjourn	*ease*	*press*
anecdotes	*focus*	*recess*
crises	*memoranda*	*slender*
doodle	*nap*	*terse*

1. The young men enjoyed listening to the old soldier's _____ about the war.

2. The spectators _____ their attention on Mary Lou Retton, the gymnast, during the 1984 Olympics.

3. Freedom of the _____ ensures that government will not censor the news.

4. Many people like to _____ while they talk on the telephone.

5. After she lost twenty pounds, she was _____ and beautiful.

6. The question directed to the speaker was long and detailed; his answer was _____.

7. Whenever she sat down to watch television, she _____ instead.

8. At 6:00 P.M., the president _____ the meeting to nine o'clock the following morning.

9. Two aspirin usually _____ a headache.

10. School children look forward to _____ at noon so that they can eat lunch and then play games.

GOSPORT, England, Nov. 12, 1807. — In this small seafaring town on Plymouth Bay there lived an attractive young woman named Harriet Magnis. She had an obsession. She wanted a baby for her hus-
5 band. Above all things on earth, she wanted a baby for Richard. But she couldn't have one.

Obsessions drive people to commit all manner of strange acts. Harriet Magnis's obsession drove her to commit one of the most bizarre crimes in history.

10 Richard was a gunner in the Royal Navy. Even though he was at sea for two or three years at a stretch, and was home for only a few days at a time, Harriet loved him deeply and her tragic failure to provide him with a child haunted her.

15 To make it worse, she feared that her husband would find some other woman on his travels, a woman who could give him what she could not, and that he would leave her forever.

But this day, as she wrote to her husband, she
20 said: "My darling, God has finally smiled on us! I am at last with child! By the time you get home again, our child will have been born and you will be the father you have always wanted to be."

Sealing the letter in an envelope, she addressed it
25 to the next port that her husband's ship would touch, and she took it to the post office.

There was only one thing wrong. Harriet wasn't pregnant. She had lied to her husband for one reason. Her letter would reach him on Christmas. And she
30 wanted to make him happy! Months passed. A letter from her absentee husband. Had the baby come? Was it a boy or a girl?

It would have saved Harriet endless grief had she now told him the truth, but she couldn't do that. It
35 would hurt him too much. So she said that the baby had come, and that it was a boy.

What she would do when her husband came home and wanted to see his son, Harriet apparently had no idea. She worried about it a good deal, then worried
40 a great deal more when she learned that her husband's ship was coming home in a few days.

When Richard's ship came in, Harriet rushed across to Portsmouth to meet him. "Where is my son?" he shouted.

45 Harriet thought fast. "Oh, my dear," she said, "I didn't expect you so soon. The doctor felt the sea air was bad for him, so I took him to stay with his grandparents in Sussex."

She knew perfectly well that Richard would be in
50 port for only a few days, not long enough for him to go to Sussex. So she was safe. For the time being.

The next time he came home, she had another excuse. Next time, still another. But he was growing suspicious. It didn't dawn on him that there wasn't
55 any child at all. He merely suspected that she was hiding the child because it was another man's. So he laid down the law to Harriet. Next time he came home, he would see his son—and no excuses would be accepted.

60 Poor Harriet! Her lies had gotten her into really deep water now. She had succeeded in deceiving him

Desire for a Child Was Nearly Tragic

by DOANE R. HOAG

at little Thomas Dellow. Incredibly, the child was not only the right age, but he actually looked remarkably like Richard Magnis!

Five minutes later Mary Cox discovered that the boy was missing. The police were informed. A nationwide search was begun, handbills distributed throughout the country. Back in Gosport, Harriet proudly took little Thomas down to Portsmouth to see his daddy's ship come in. And how delighted Richard was! A son! At last! For the few days of his shore leave, he lived in ecstasy, never dreaming the truth. Then he went off to sea again, still not knowing.

But after he left, Harriet became panicky, especially when the neighbors began to ask questions about the sudden appearance of her "child" and even more so when the wanted notices appeared in the local post office.

Filled with fear and remorse now, she took little Thomas Dellow back to London, left him in front of a police station and fled. Then she sat down and wrote a long tearful letter to her husband, telling him the truth at last.

In due time the letter was delivered to Richard's ship, but not to him. In his anxiety to see his little son again, Richard had jumped ship and gone A.W.O.L. His wife's letter, admitting everything, was delivered to the captain of the ship instead of to Richard. Thinking it might provide some clue to Richard's absence, he opened it . . . .

Harriet Magnis was arrested and held for trial at the Hampshire Assizes. But there the judge decided that since the crime had not been committed in Hampshire, but in London, the court had no jurisdiction. So Harriet was discharged and never tried again.

The judge may have understood a little better than anyone else. His own wife was also unable to bear children. She, too, had an obsession. But instead of stealing someone else's child, she had committed suicide.

for three years, but now she knew that she either had to produce a 3-year-old boy who looked like Richard, or have to spill the whole truth to him.

So Harriet embarked upon a fantastic scheme. She would steal a child.

There was no possibility of finding just what she wanted in the little town of Gosport, so she went to London. There, day after day, she tramped through the streets looking for the child she had to have.

At the same time, a Mrs. Charles Dellow went to London to see her doctor, taking her two children with her: a little girl, Mary, five, and a boy, Thomas, three. As she reached the doctor's office, she left the children in the greengrocer's shop downstairs. The grocer's wife, Mary Cox, promised to watch them.

Fifteen minutes later Harriet Magnis came by, paused at the door. There she stopped short, staring

VOCABULARY LIST

obsession *(n.)* idea that occupies one's mind continually

bizarre *(adj.)* odd; strange

haunt *(v.)* to return to the mind often

port *(n.)* town or place where ships load or unload

pregnant *(adj.)* having a child developing in the body

suspicious *(adj.)* thinking (a person) guilty without proof

deceive *(v.)* to cause someone to believe something that is false

embark *(v.)* **upon** to start

scheme *(n.)* plan, sometimes secret

handbill *(n.)* printed sheet handed out to people

ecstasy *(n.)* great joy, happiness

remorse *(n.)* feeling of being sorry that one has done wrong

A.W.O.L. military abbreviation for Absent Without Official Leave (permission)

clue *(n.)* guide to the solving of a mystery or problem

jurisdiction *(n.)* legal authority or power

assizes *(n.)* (until 1971) periodical sessions of court held in each county of England

try *(v.)* **(in a court of law)** to determine in a court of law the guilt or innocence of (a person)

suicide *(n.)* killing of oneself on purpose

commit suicide *(v.; n.)* to kill oneself on purpose

Additional Vocabulary

kidnap *(v.)* to steal (a child); carry off (a person) by force

hijack *(v.)* to steal a moving vehicle (airplane, bus, etc.)

Reading Comprehension

MULTIPLE CHOICE

Choose the correct answers.

_____ 1. All the events in the foregoing selection took place in
   A. the twentieth century.
   B. London.
   C. the last century.
   D. New Hampshire.

_____ 2. Harriet didn't see her husband for long periods of time because
   A. he had a sweetheart in every port.
   B. he worked for a shipping company.
   C. he was angry with her for not having a child.
   D. he was in the British Navy.

_____ 3. Harriet deceived her husband
   A. for a few days.
   B. twice.
   C. for three years.
   D. forever.

_____ 4. Richard suspected that
   A. Harriet had never been pregnant.
   B. he was not the father of Harriet's child.
   C. Harriet had kidnapped a child.
   D. Harriet's obsession had driven her crazy.

_____ 5. Harriet's obsession drove her
   A. to commit suicide.
   B. to steal.
   C. to leave her husband.
   D. to move to London.

_____ 6. The child whom Harriet presented to Richard was
   A. her own.
   B. the grocer's.
   C. Mrs. Dellow's.
   D. Mary Cox's.

_____ 7. Richard jumped ship because
   A. he learned what Harriet had done.
   B. the police were looking for him.
   C. he loved his wife.
   D. he loved Thomas.

_____ 8. The first person to find out the truth about Harriet's bizarre crime was
A. the captain of the ship.
B. Harriet's lawyer.
C. the judge.
D. Richard.

_____ 9. Harriet was not punished for her crime because
A. Thomas was returned to his real mother.
B. the judge felt sorry for Harriet.
C. the crime was committed in London.
D. Richard forgave his wife.

_____ 10. The judge's wife, like Harriet, had
A. kidnapped a child.
B. not been able to have children.
C. committed suicide.
D. been arrested.

Activities: Writing a Summary and Your Own Ending to the Story

Read "Desire for a Child . . ." carefully again. Look for the *main idea* and *the essential details*. Write a **summary**—a short account—of the story. (*Remember:* A summary should be *brief* and *in your own words*.)

What do you think happened to Harriet and Richard? Did they live happily ever after? Write your own ending to the story, and if you wish, read it to your classmates.

Idioms

Sometimes you can *guess* the meaning of an idiom from its **context**—*what comes before and after the idiom*.

MULTIPLE CHOICE

Read the following excerpts from the selection, and then choose the appropriate meaning of each of the underlined idioms.

_____ 1. "Even though he was at sea for <u>two or three years at a stretch</u>, and was home for only a few days at a time . . . ." (lines 10–12)
A. every two or three years
B. two or three years continuously
C. every other year

_____ 2. "She worried about it <u>a good deal</u>, then worried a great deal more when she learned that her husband's ship was coming home in a few days." (lines 39–41)
A. from time to time   C. quite a lot
B. somewhat

_____ 3. "She knew . . . that Richard would be in port for only a few days, not long enough for him to go to Sussex. So she was safe. <u>For the time being</u>." (lines 49–51)
A. For the present   C. Forever
B. For the future

_____ 4. "But he was growing suspicious. <u>It didn't dawn on him</u> that there wasn't any child at all. He merely suspected that she was hiding the child because it was another man's." (lines 53–56)
A. It didn't matter to him
B. The next morning he suspected
C. It didn't become clear to him

_____ 5. "So he <u>laid down the law to Harriet</u>. Next time he came home, he would see his son—and no excuses would be accepted." (lines 56–59)
A. threatened to take Harriet to court
B. gave strict orders to Harriet
C. threatened to put Harriet in jail

_____ 6. "Poor Harriet! Her lies had gotten her into <u>really deep water</u> now." (lines 60–61)
A. a lot of trouble
B. the ocean
C. jail

_____ 7. "In his anxiety to see his little son again, Richard <u>had jumped ship</u> and gone A.W.O.L." (lines 103–105)
A. had resigned from the Navy
B. had deserted the ship
C. had told the captain he was leaving the ship

Vocabulary

SUFFIXES	A **suffix** is a syllable or syllables added to the end of a word to form a new word. For example: the suffix *-ful* (full of; causing) added to the word *pain* = *painful* (causing pain). The suffix *-less* (without) added to the word *pain* = *painless* (without pain).

Notice that *pain* is a **noun** and that *painful* and *painless* are **adjectives**. The suffixes *-ful* and *-less* are called **adjective suffixes** because they change nouns into adjectives.

Part 1

*Look at the two examples in the exercise below and then form new words (**adjectives**) by adding the suffixes **-ful** and **-less** to the appropriate nouns. (Note: end + ful ≠ a word.)*

	Noun	Adjective	Adjective
Example:	end	—	*endless* (line 33)
Example:	tear	*tearful* (line 100)	*tearless*
	pain		
	child	—	
	thought*		
	hope		
	spot	—	
	home	—	
	power		
	worth	—	
	rest		
	harm		

---

* Consult your English-English dictionary for definitions of the adjectives.

Note: The suffix *-ly* changes many **adjectives** into **adverbs:**
   She *tearfully* told her friend the bad news.
   He *thoughtlessly* dropped cigarette ashes on her carpet.

Part 2

*Fill in the blanks in the following sentences with the appropriate **new**
words you have formed.*

1. Her kitchen was so _____ you could eat off the floor.
2. Too much sun is _____ to the skin.
3. Thousands of people were left _____ after the earth-
    quake.
4. The United States and Russia are the most _____
    nations in the world.
5. The politician's speech was so boring it seemed _____.
6. It was very _____ of you to remember my birth-
    day.
7. Going to the dentist can be a _____ experience.
8. Anyone who deliberately parks his car in a space reserved for the
    handicapped is very _____.
9. We finally got away from the city and spent a _____
    weekend in the mountains.
10. Although the doctor said Jim's heart condition was _____,
    his family was _____ that he would recover.
11. Many _____ couples want to adopt children.
12. He paid a thousand dollars for a painting that he later found out
    was _____.
13. I had a _____ night because I was worried about final
    exams.

You have learned that the verbs *count, run,* and *get,* when combined with certain particles, change their meanings. The same is true of the verb *look:*

$$look + after = to \ take \ care \ of$$
$$look + over = to \ examine$$

Study the two-word verbs and their definitions listed below, and then fill in each blank in the following sentences with the appropriate two-word verb (and preposition, if necessary). Be sure to use the correct tense of the verb.

look after   to take care of

look for   to search for (line 70)

look forward to*   to expect with pleasure

look like   to resemble (lines 80–81)

look out *(for)*   to be careful; watch out (for)

look over *(S)*   to examine; inspect

look up *(S)*   (1) to find (an address, a word, a telephone number); (2) to visit

look up to*   to respect

look down on*   to have a low opinion of someone

1. Would you please _____ my term paper and tell me if there are any spelling errors?

2. When her mother goes to work, she has to _____ her baby sister.

3. Alcoholism is a disease; we must not _____ a person who has a drinking problem.

_____

* three-word verbs

4. Amy went to the library and _____ the word in the unabridged dictionary.

5. When you go to Athens, Georgia, be sure to _____ my friend who is a student at the University of Georgia.

6. _____ cars when you cross Briarcliff Road!

7. Athletes should always behave well since many children _____ _____ them.

8. All winter I _____ warm weather; now I miss the snowy days of January.

9. While we _____ our cat, she was sitting on top of the fence watching us.

10. Mark thinks he _____ his father, but we think he _____ his mother.

Review: Phrasal Verbs with *Get* and *Look*

DIALOGUE COMPLETION

Complete these conversations using phrasal verbs with **get** or **look**. Then practice the conversations aloud with a partner. Follow the example.

1. YOU: I didn't see you on the bus this morning.
   FRIEND: *I got off before you got on.*

2. YOU: I thought you were still out of town.
   FRIEND: _____

3. YOU: Welcome back to work. What arrangements did you make for your baby?
   FRIEND: _____

4. YOU: I've finished reading the passage but don't know what several of the words mean.

   FRIEND: _____

5. YOU: You and your sisters are all very pretty young ladies.

   FRIEND: _____

6. YOU: Congratulations on your new job! What are your hours?

   FRIEND: _____

7. YOU: Are you doing anything exciting next summer?

   FRIEND: _____

8. YOU: Do you have to go to that meeting? Let's go to a movie.

   FRIEND: _____

9. YOU: Jack has lost three jobs this year. Do you have any idea why he can't keep a job?

   FRIEND: _____

10. YOU: What does Mrs. Cohen say we should always do before we hand in a test?

    FRIEND: _____

MULTIPLE MEANINGS

Miss
(v.)

You have learned that a word can have more than one meaning. The verb *miss* has several meanings:

1. to fail (be unable) to hit
2. to fail to catch, attend, find
3. to fail to find the answer to
4. to notice the absence of
5. to feel sorry that someone is absent

*The following passage contains <u>six different phrases</u> that can be re-placed by the verb **miss.** On a separate sheet of paper, rewrite the passage, substituting the correct form of **miss** for each of the six phrases.*

I overslept this morning and was unable to catch the bus to the university. (I haven't slept well lately because I want to see my parents very much. They're still in Japan.) My classmate picked me up in her car later in the morning. Although I had moved to another street, I told her she couldn't fail to find my house; it was painted bright yellow and had a red front door.

As soon as we got to school, I explained to my teacher why I had not been in reading class. She returned my last test; I was very upset to see that I had incorrectly answered six questions.

My friend and I then went to the cafeteria for lunch. When I opened my purse to pay for my meal, I didn't see my wallet. It dawned on me that this wasn't my lucky day!

**Missing
(adj.)**

The adjective *missing* means *not to be found; gone.*

1. ". . . Mary Cox discovered that the boy was *missing*." (lines 82–83)
2. The first three pages of the book are *missing*.

Note: **Miss** is a title of respect used before the name of an unmarried woman: *Miss Jones.*
Mrs. (<u>mis</u>iz, <u>miz</u>iz) is a title of respect used before the name of a married woman: *Mrs. Smith.*
Ms. (miz) is a title of respect used before the name of a married or an unmarried woman: *Ms. Jones, Ms. Smith.*

Miss versus Lose

*Non-native speakers of English sometimes confuse **miss** and **lose**. Look up **lose** in your English-English dictionary and study its various meanings. Then fill in each blank in the following letter with either **miss** or **lose**. Use correct verb tenses.*

Sunday P.M.

Dearest Joan,

    Your plane left just two hours ago and I already ＿＿＿＿＿ you! I'm sorry you ＿＿＿＿＿＿ the earlier flight; I always ＿＿＿＿ my way when I ＿＿＿＿ the exit to the airport.

    You look very beautiful and slender. I'm happy you ＿＿＿＿ those ten pounds because *you* wanted to; I never thought you were overweight.

    I forgot to tell you that my company is in financial trouble. About 250 employees have ＿＿＿＿ their jobs. I don't think I'll be fired.

    I'm going to the baseball game tomorrow night. If the Braves ＿＿＿＿, I'll be in deep water! I bet one hundred dollars on their—the Braves'—winning, and I can't afford to ＿＿＿＿ that much money.

    Try not to ＿＿＿＿ any classes during the week before final exams. And get up early so that you won't ＿＿＿＿ breakfast.

    Will call you in a day or two.

I love you,
Mickey

P.S. My friend John called to tell me he ＿＿＿＿ his parents in a tragic automobile accident. I'm so sorry.

Fill in the blanks in the following sentences with the appropriate words from the list below. Use correct verb tenses.

bizarre	*hijack*	*remorse*
clue	*kidnap*	*schemes*
ecstasy	*obsession*	*stare*
excuses	*panicky*	*suspicious*

1. The president's _____ was the fear that he might be assassinated at any moment.

2. When the beautiful actress entered the room, everybody stopped talking and _____ at her.

3. People became _____ when a large number of _____ murders were committed in their city.

4. The criminals who _____ the rich man's child demanded a ransom of one million dollars.

5. If you're walking alone at night, be _____ of anyone who seems to be following you.

6. He was in _____ every time she looked at him with her beautiful brown eyes!

7. His _____ for making a lot of money quickly and easily were always unsuccessful.

8. Two men and a woman _____ an airplane and demanded that the pilot take them to a distant city.

9. The police were not able to find a single _____ to help them solve the crime.

10. He later felt _____ that he had not taken the advice of his parents.

11. My teacher refused to accept any more _____ for my being late to class every day.

Sylvia Porter is an authority on money matters. (Her columns appear in more than 400 newspapers and she is the author of seven books.) In the following excerpt from Sylvia Porter's New Money Book for the 80's, *Ms. Porter advises college students to* plan *their* spending, *to have a* budget. *If you are having a hard time managing your money, perhaps this is the right time to start a budget.*

Now let's assume you're a college student living—or trying to live—on an allowance. How can the money management plan help you?

Some of you are at home during school years and
5 are on weekly allowances; many others of you live away and receive your checks every month. But for all of you the problem is identical: college years are a constant—and usually losing—battle to make financial ends meet.

10 Halfway through the week or month, most of you are either broke or on the brink. Some of you live high the first few days you get your money, then scramble for help toward the end. Some of you have only far-apart intervals when you are out of debt.
15 The vast majority of you are either flush or frantic.

But your allowance is a paycheck. It deserves the respect and care you will give a paycheck after graduation. Just as your parents get the most from their dollars by living by certain financial rules, so you in
20 college can get the greatest satisfaction out of your allowance if you live by certain financial rules.

Whether you live at home or away from home, whether you're at the fanciest of schools or on a scholarship or working your way through, the fun-
25 damental principles of money management apply equally.

Here are your "Allowance ABC's." Try them for size.

(1) Plan the spending of your allowance with
30 your parents before you leave for college, and then keep planning on your own from the day you arrive at school.

It's nonsense to say that $40 a week will be fine when $40 a week won't do at all for what you have
35 to cover. Plan realistically and with a clear understanding of what your allowance is to take care of. Then, when you arrive at school, work out your day-to-day budget to cover your necessities and luxuries. Be honest with yourself. (If Cokes and coffee are
40 going to cost X cents a day, plan for X cents a day.) If your allowance is supposed to cover such items as new panty hose, dry cleaning, shoe repair, oil, gas, auto maintenance, and so forth, budget these costs—

Budgeting If You're in College

by SYLVIA PORTER

don't ignore them. This is *your* budget; it should fit
45 *you.*

(2) Deposit your money in a bank account and
draw on it only as you need the money. If you carry
a wad of cash with you, you'll risk being mugged and
the temptation to spend it recklessly may become
50 irresistible. Discipline yourself via your bank account; the lessons you learn now will be valuable
throughout your life . . . .

(3) If you and your parents can manage it, also
start an account in a nearby savings bank, or try to
55 build one through the term . . . .

(4) Don't figure down to pennies. No money plan
ever should be that precise. For your protection and
pleasure, give yourself a margin of safety.

(5) Keep some simple records to show you where
60 your allowance is going and why . . . . For one week,

list on a sheet of paper what you spend and where
and when you spend it. See how this week's total fits
into the monthly total allotted to you. If need be,
push your spending around to make it fit. When
65 you've found the right pattern, stick with it. Keep
your list in a convenient spot where you will see it
from day to day.

(6) Stretch your dollars by learning how to buy
items you must have (toiletries, for instance) during
70 special sales or in economy sizes, etc. If you're buying
your own wardrobe, stretch your dollars further by
buying simple basic styles which will last longer and
cost least in upkeep. Also investigate how easy it will
be for you to save by pooling purchases with your
75 friends so you can buy in bulk at bargain prices.

(7) If your evidence is clear after a trial that your
funds are too limited, renegotiate your allowance.
Your records will be your evidence.

DENNIS THE MENACE   by Hank Ketcham

*"MY MOM IS IN THE OTHER ROOM
TRYING TO MAKE ENDS MEET."*

VOCABULARY LIST

budget *(n.)*   plan of how to spend one's money

budget *(v.)*   to plan how to spend one's money

assume *(v.)*   to suppose

allowance *(n.)*   money provided regularly

broke *(adj.)*   without money

vast *(adj.)*   very large

flush *(adj.)*   having plenty of money

frantic *(adj.)*   very anxious, afraid

rule *(n.)*   statement about how things are to be done

nonsense *(n.)*   foolish talk or acts

luxury *(n.)*   something not necessary that gives enjoyment

ignore *(v.)*   to refuse to pay attention to

wad *(n.)*   large roll (of paper money)

mug *(v.) (slang)*   to attack and rob someone

reckless *(adj.)*   careless

irresistible *(adj.)*   too pleasant to be resisted (fought against)

toiletry *(n.)*   any article used in cleaning or grooming oneself
(toothpaste, soap, perfume, etc.)

upkeep *(n.)*   cost of keeping something in good condition

wardrobe *(n.)*   all the clothing belonging to one person

renegotiate *(v.)*   to talk over and arrange again

Reading Comprehension

TRUE/FALSE STATEMENTS

Answer the following statements True or False.

_____ 1. According to Sylvia Porter, students have a difficult time handling money.

_____ 2. Ms. Porter says an allowance is like a salary.

_____ 3. Only college students can benefit from a budget.

_____ 4. A budget should cover popcorn and movies as well as bread and meat.

_____ 5. The more cash you carry, the more you'll spend.

_____ 6. You can save money by buying old-fashioned clothes.

_____ 7. A twelve-ounce jar of instant coffee will stretch your dollar more than a four-ounce jar.

_____ 8. "Toiletries" are for bathroom use only.

_____ 9. Never ask your parents for a bigger allowance.

_____ 10. One can conclude from the selection that a budget is a set of financial rules that a person makes for himself.

Vocabulary

SUBSTITUTION: WORDS & IDIOMS

On a separate sheet of paper, rewrite the following paragraphs, substituting the appropriate words or idioms from the reading selection for the underlined parts of the sentences.

According to Sylvia Porter, college students are always afraid they won't have enough money to live on.* At times they're completely without money or very nearly without any. After receiving their allowances, they live well for a while, but later on in the week or month, they are hurriedly looking around for financial help. The intervals during which some students don't owe money are few and far between.

Ms. Porter offers some basic rules for managing an allowance. These rules apply not only to students who attend the best and most costly schools but to students who must have jobs in order to attend school.

(1) Keep a weekly record of what you spend; then plan your spending. If you're satisfied with your budget, continue to use it!

(2) Have available some money beyond what you need for emergencies or pleasure.

(3) Get the most for your money. For example, you and your friends share what you buy so that you can buy in large quantities, thereby saving money.

---

    * *Example:* According to Sylvia Porter, college students are always afraid they won't be able to make ends meet.

Fill in the blanks in the following sentences with the appropriate words from the list below. Use correct verb tenses.

allowance   ignore   renegotiate
assume   irresistible   rules
broke (adj.)   luxury   upkeep
flush   nonsense   vast
frantic   reckless   wardrobe

1. A winter _____ should include a warm coat.

2. One must consider not only the cost of a car, but its _____.

3. _____ drivers cause accidents.

4. In order to play a game, one must know the _____.

5. Those people who find food _____ are usually overweight.

6. Traveling is a _____ most people can't afford.

7. After paying all his bills, he discovered he was _____.

8. To _____ the warning about cancer on a cigarette package is both foolish and dangerous.

9. After five years, the two countries _____ the treaty.

10. The parents were _____ as they searched for their lost child.

11. We sometimes _____ that no news is good news.

12. It's _____ to think that marijuana is a harmless drug.

13. A _____ number of people in the United States are illiterate.

14. The only time Maria was _____ was the same day she received her _____ from her father!

Abigail Van Buren and her twin sister, Ann Landers, are both advice columnists who have helped thousands of troubled people solve their personal problems. "Dear Ann" and "Dear Abby" appear in many newspapers throughout the world. None of the letters in these columns are made up; they were written by real people with real problems.

Ann Landers

Abigail Van Buren

1 **DEAR ABBY:** I am writing to you about a problem that may seem trivial to you, but it is threatening to destroy my marriage. My husband does everything in twos. If we go to a restaurant once, we have to go back there a second time even if we don't like the place!

We have two children and own two homes. My husband insists that we attend every movie, ballet, opera and concert twice!

Four years ago we took an around-the-world tour. Now my husband wants to do it again! Abby, we can't afford it. This man is driving me crazy, and I have told him that unless he gets professional help I am going to leave him. Am I wrong? Or is he in need of help? He agreed to listen to you. If you print this, no names, please. He owns two businesses.

—**"J" IN CHICAGO**

DEAR J.: Your "two-timer" husband has a compulsive neurosis. My psychiatric consultant says it is some kind of "ritual" he's obsessed with, and he should see a therapist who practices behavioral therapy. Consult your local mental health clinic or the American Psychiatric Association for recommendations. (P.S. Better get the names of two doctors.)

2 **DEAR ABBY:** I just turned 15. I had a baby girl in May of this year. The baby's father is 16. He said he would marry me, but I wasn't ready to get married at the time, and I'm still not. He is in no position to be a husband and father either.

I had plans to put the baby up for adoption, but I changed my mind. The baby is under temporary foster care now, and there will be a court hearing in September, so I have to make up my mind.

My parents want nothing to do with this baby. They think I should put it up for adoption. I really want to keep her, but the people at the welfare department are giving me a hard time. They don't think I'm capable of taking on so much responsibility at my age.

They may be right, but I think I would like to try. Please tell me what to do. —**ALL TORN UP**

DEAR TORN: You need much more help than I can give you in this column. Expert counseling is available to you without cost from your local Planned Parenthood chapter, Family Service Association or mental health clinic. Please call one of those facilities (they are listed in your directory) and tell them Abby suggested you call.

Advice from Abby and Ann

by ABIGAIL VAN BUREN and ANN LANDERS

You have already shown mature judgment by refusing a hasty marriage and considering adoption for the child.

You need to sort out your thoughts, plan for your future and then decide what will be best for the baby and yourself. I have confidence in your ability to make the right decision. Good luck and God bless. And please let me hear from you again. I care.

3   **DEAR ABBY:** I am a shoplifter. I started out as a teen-ager by taking small, inexpensive items, and I always got away with it. I kept telling myself it would be the last time, but I just couldn't stop. I prayed to God to help me stop, and I thought I had because I didn't take anything for over a year. Then it happened again. I just had to take something! As I was walking out of the store, I was stopped and caught with something marked $1.99 but ended up paying

a $60 fine plus the hurt to my family, myself and mostly to God.

I have promised God and myself that I will never again steal as much as one bobby pin, and I think now I can keep that promise.

This letter is for everyone who thinks it is not so bad to shoplift an item or two. Never start! It can get to be a habit or a game, and it's hard to stop. Please correct my mistakes in spelling, Abby, but print this. It may help someone. Thank you. Sign me . . .   **—SHOPLIFTER**

DEAR SHOPLIFTER: You have paid the price, so drop the label. There is a lot of good in one who wants to help others through his own unfortunate experiences. Thanks for writing, and God bless.

4   **DEAR ABBY:** I'm 70 and have been a widow for two years. My husband owned a tavern and we both worked there. Lou, a regular tavern customer, started coming around to see me right after my husband died, and we really got stuck on each other. Lou is 55 and knows my real age, but says he doesn't care about the age difference—he loves me anyway.

Now the problem. I fix him supper every night, but this love affair doesn't seem to be going anywhere because Lou has to be home every night by midnight. He says he lives with his sister, who's 62, and his mother, 83, and they need a man in the house. I've never been to his house or met his mother and his sister. He says they're kind of weird and not very sociable.

Abby, I just sold my tavern and I want to get married and travel some. Lou doesn't want me to go with any other men.

What should I do? Lou says I should give him more time. How much time should I give him?
—TIRED OF WAITING

DEAR TIRED: Until tomorrow. Tell him you don't care how "weird" his mother and sister are, you want to meet them anyway. And if he doesn't arrange a meeting pronto, kiss him goodbye.

5 **DEAR ABBY:** I'm sitting here with a terrible headache and an upset stomach because I can't remember where I put my money, and a payment is due today at the bank!

I'm only 35, but my memory is so bad I'm ashamed of myself. Four years ago I hid some jewelry before going out one night. I still haven't found it.

I order things and forget to pick them up. I forget to make phone calls. I forget where I park my car. But I remember petty things like an argument I had with my husband 10 years ago. So why can't I remember everyday things?

Writing notes to myself doesn't help. I forget where I put the notes.

I've thought about going to the local mental health clinic, but I have a friend who works there and I'd just die if she found out how dumb I am.

Are there others like myself? What do they do about it? **—FORGETFUL FRAN**

DEAR FRAN: There are MANY like yourself. The wise ones get professional help, which is what you should do. Call your mental health clinic for 'an appointment.

6 **DEAR ABBY:** I am 19, and I'm dating a 27-year-old man. My parents do not object to the age difference because there's a 20-year difference in their ages. The problem is that my parents think this man is not good-looking enough for me!

I love him very much and he loves me, but my parents are terribly disappointed that I didn't pick a better-looking fellow. He's not really bad-looking, Abby. He is about an inch shorter than I am and he's losing his hair, but I don't care. He treats me better than any guy I've ever gone with, and our relationship is great!

Whenever I go out with him, my mother puts on a long face and says she hopes I'm not "serious" about him. I tell her I AM serious about him, and then she looks so sad and shakes her head as if to say, "You must be nuts."

Both she and Dad are nagging me and making me feel guilty for loving a man whose looks don't come up to their expectations. I need advice. By the way, I'm no beauty myself.

    —S. IN ENGLISHTOWN, N.J.

DEAR S: Tune your parents out and listen to your heart. If you love him and he treats you well, pay no attention to what anyone says. Handsome is as handsome does.

7 **DEAR ANN LANDERS:** My husband and I have been arguing over something since we married five years ago.

Ed is from a family of eight boys and one girl. His mother was widowed and wants to live with us and bring her 35-year-old son who is emotionally unstable. He can't work, although he is in excellent physical condition.

Ed travels in his job. If his mother and brother move in, I'll be their maid and chauffeur. Also, we would be their sole support. Ed's mother and brother have an apartment but my husband thinks it is his duty to take them in. I've told him it would break up our marriage. (My mother-in-law is very strong-minded and has to run everything.)

We have two young children and are trying to get on our feet financially. Ed says I am selfish.

I insist that each of the nine children should contribute toward an apartment for their mother and brother so the burden will not fall on one. I love my husband and do not want to divorce him, but I cannot go along with his notion that we accept all the responsibility.

Please settle this. He says he will abide by your opinion. **—DESPERATE IN TEXAS**

DEAR D. IN T.: My "decision" appears in your letter. "Each child should contribute toward an apartment for mother and brother so the burden will not fall on one person."

DEAR ANN LANDERS: Please don't laugh at me. I am very serious and need some of your best advice. I am a girl who will be 15 in seven weeks. A certain boy I like a lot is going to ask me for a date any minute. I can just feel it in my bones.

The problem is I wear glasses. I'm expecting him to kiss me goodnight. He wears glasses, too, and sometimes when both parties wear glasses, kissing can be awkward. Should I remove my glasses when we get to the door, in preparation for the kiss—or would it look too planned? If I took off my glasses and he didn't kiss me I'd fall right through the porch.

Please rush your answer, Ann. This is an emergency. **—TOODIE**

DEAR TOODIE: I am typing as fast as I can, honey. I hope the advice reaches you in time.

Glasses will not interfere with a goodnight kiss—even if both parties are wearing them. It may take a little tilting of the head and jockeying for position but you'll manage, I'm sure. Others have.

VOCABULARY LIST

advice (n.)   opinion about what should be done

advise (v.)   to give advice to

trivial (adj.)   of very little importance

compulsive neurosis (adj.; n.)   mental disorder in which the person feels forced to engage in a particular behavior over and over again

ritual (rich ü əl) (n.)   any behavior repeated in a certain manner

behavioral therapy (adj.; n.)   treatment used to change the behavior of a person suffering from a mental disorder

adoption (n.)   taking of a child (legally) as one's own

foster (adj.)   giving or receiving parental care though not by kin or related legally

petty (adj.)   having little importance; trivial

nag (v.)   to find fault with (a person) all the time; to annoy with persistent demands or complaints

burden (n.)   serious responsibility

abide (v.)   to agree to

awkward (adj.)   clumsy; not graceful

tilting (n.)   leaning; slanting

jockeying (for position) (n.)   attempting to get a better position

Reading Comprehension

QUESTIONS AND DISCUSSION

Answer the following questions.

1. Of the eight people who wrote to Abby and Ann, who do you think has the most serious problem? The least serious problem?
2. Do Abby and Ann think they are capable of solving all kinds of problems? Explain.
3. Do you think parents should tell their adult children whom to date? Why or why not? Which letter deals with this question? Why do the writer's parents object to their daughter's boyfriend? Explain Abby's answer: "Tune your parents out and listen to your heart . . . . Handsome is as handsome does."
4. Do you think a woman should marry a man much younger than she? Give your reasons. Is "age" the problem in Letter 4? What *is* the problem? What is Abby's advice?
5. Which letter was written by an unwed mother? What options (choices) does the young mother have in solving her problem? What does *she* want to do? What is Abby's advice? What advice would *you* give this young girl?
6. Which writer is not seeking advice? Why did she write Abby? (How do you know the writer is a woman? Find the clue.) Explain Abby's answer: "You have paid the price, so drop the label . . . ."
7. Why does "Desperate in Texas" think she won't be able to get along with her mother-in-law? Where does Ann find the solution to this woman's problem? What is the solution? Do young people in your country live with their parents after marriage, and if so, do you think this is a good idea? Explain your answer.
8. Why is one writer's husband "driving her crazy"? What has the writer threatened to do? What is Abby's advice?
9. What advice would you give "Toodie"?
10. Why do you think people write to Abby and Ann for advice? Whom do *you* ask for advice when you have a problem?

Activity: Making a Brief Oral Report

Go to the library and read several more letters to Abby or Ann in the newspapers there. (The index on the front page of the newspaper will indicate the page number.) Be prepared to tell your classmates about the most interesting letter and the advice that Abby or Ann gives to the writer.

Idioms

MEANING FROM CONTEXT

*Read the letter at the beginning of the chapter in which each of the following idioms appears. Try to guess the **meaning** of the idiom from its **context**.*

1. "I just turned fifteen." (Letter 2)

   _____

2. "Lou . . . started coming around to see me right after my husband died, and we really *got stuck on each other*." (Letter 4)

   _____

3. "Whenever I go out with him, my mother *puts on a long face . . . .*" (Letter 6)

   _____

4. "I tell her I AM serious about him, and then she . . . shakes her head as if to say, *'You must be nuts.'*" (Letter 6)

   _____

5. "My mother-in-law is very strong-minded and has *to run everything.*" (Letter 7)

   _____

6. "We . . . are trying *to get on our feet financially.*" (Letter 7)

   _____

7. "I can just feel it in my bones." (Letter 8)

   _____

Vocabulary

MULTIPLE MEANINGS

The words **fine, sole,** and **date** all have multiple meanings. In each of the following sentences, determine the **meaning** of the underlined word from its **context.** Determine the **part of speech** of the <u>underlined</u> word by its use in the sentence.

Fine

1. "I was stopped and caught with something marked $1.99 but ended up paying a $60 <u>fine</u> . . . ." (Letter 3)

   Meaning: _____

   Part of speech: _____

2. Sometimes dust is so <u>fine</u> that we don't notice it until we begin to sneeze.

   Meaning: _____

   Part of speech: _____

3. Alonso always feels <u>fine</u> because he runs three miles every day and lifts weights several times a week.

   Meaning: _____

   Part of speech: _____

4. What a <u>fine</u> day to take a leisurely walk through the park.

   Meaning: _____

   Part of speech: _____

5. I enjoy writing with a pen that has a <u>fine</u> point.

   Meaning: _____

   Part of speech: _____

Sole

1. "Also, we would be their <u>sole</u> support." (Letter 7)

   Meaning: _____

   Part of speech: _____

2. If you're looking for comfort, buy a pair of shoes with rubber <u>soles</u>.

   Meaning: _____

   Part of speech: _____

3. That seafood restaurant serves delicious <u>sole</u>.

   Meaning: _____

   Part of speech: _____

4. People who never walk barefoot have tender <u>soles</u>.

   Meaning: _____

   Part of speech: _____

Date

1. "A certain boy I like a lot is going to ask me for a <u>date</u> any minute."
   (Letter 8)

   Meaning: _____

   Part of speech: _____

2. I forgot to <u>date</u> the check I wrote yesterday.

   Meaning: _____

   Part of speech: _____

3. Instead of eating candy between meals, try raisins, <u>dates</u>, or figs.

   Meaning: _____

   Part of speech: _____

Now look in your English-English dictionary and see if your answers are correct.

KUDZU by Doug Marlette

Panel 1: DEAR PREACHER, SHOULD I KISS ON MY FIRST DATE? CAUTIOUS

Panel 2: Dear Cautious, To each his own...

Panel 3: ..but with dates, figs and most fruits or vegetables I suggest washing 'em first.

TWO-WORD VERBS

Study the two-word verbs listed below; note how they are used in the letters to "Abby" and "Ann". Fill in the blank or blanks in each of the following sentences with the appropriate two-word verb (and preposition, if necessary) from the list. Be sure to use the correct verb tense in each sentence.

make up (one's mind) *(S)* to decide (Letter 2)

make up (a story, excuse, etc.) *(S)* to invent

make up to become friendly again after an argument

make up (a test, etc.) *(S)* to take a test that one has missed.

make up *(S)* to apply cosmetics

get away with* to do something wrong and escape punishment (Letter 3)

go with (someone) to date someone regularly (Letter 4)

pick up *(S)* (1) to go get something and return with it (Letter 5); (2) to lift; (3) to take into a car

find out *(S)* to learn, discover (Letter 5)

break up *(S)* to put an end to (Letter 7)

break up *(intransitive)* to come to an end

break down to stop functioning properly

break in *(intransitive);* **break into** *(transitive)* to enter by force

break out (1) to start suddenly (wars, fires, etc.); (2) to have pimples, rashes on the skin

go along (with) to agree (with) (Letter 7)

---

* Three-word verb

1. Before I go home, I have to _____ the birthday cake. I ordered from Ray's Bakery.

2. They _____ each other four years before they got married.

3. When the fire _____, no one was at home.

4. I don't think students should _____ cheating.

5. The same burglar _____ several homes last night.

6. During adolescence the skin is more likely to _____.

7. Children nowadays like to _____ stories about extra-terrestrial playmates.

8. All your clothes are on the floor; please _____ them _____ before you leave home.

9. Christina and her husband didn't speak to each other for three days, but then they kissed and _____.

10. Please _____ Martha _____ on your way to school.

11. Maria _____ that she had to score 550 on the TOEFL in order to enter the graduate school of her choice.

12. All the dishes are dirty because the dishwasher _____
_____.

13. The people _____ everything the president said in his speech except his proposal to increase taxes.

14. James and his wife seemed so happy that everyone was shocked when they _____.

15. She can't _____ her mind about what courses to take next quarter.

16. If you miss a test, Professor Greenleaf will not let you _____ it _____.

At some future time, you will probably have a job interview. In the following excerpt from Job Hunting Secrets & Tactics,* *the author lists some "dos" and "don'ts" to remember when that day comes. The author writes, "A good point to remember as you read the list is that no single* do *will get you the job. But any one of the* don'ts *could disqualify you."*

DON'TS

Don't be late. In fact, plan to be 10 to 15 minutes early for any scheduled interview. If you are late or arrive just in the nick of time, the interviewer will start to wonder how prompt you might be after you
5   start to work.

Don't wear your outer clothes into an interview. Take any kind of overcoat or topcoat off. Take rubber boots off and leave them in the employment lobby. Wearing those into an interview gives the impression
10 that you are anxious to leave.

Don't sit down until you are asked. Don't worry about this. The recruiter won't make you stand, but if you move quickly to your chair and sit down, you will appear forward.

* The information in this chapter applies equally to interviewers and applicants of both sexes.

15   *Don't* have anything in your mouth except your teeth—no gum, no candies, no breath mints; in fact, don't smoke during the first interview; it is distracting to everyone.

Don't lean on or put your elbows on the interview-
20 er's desk. Sit back in your chair, so the interviewer can see more of you. Sit erect.

Don't wear sunglasses into an interview, and if you don't wear your eyeglasses all the time, don't park them on top of your head (some candidates actually
25 do that). Take them off and put them in your purse or pocket.

Don't carry an oversized handbag even if it is fashionable. Carry a bag that is smaller and more manageable. Put it on the floor during the interview, or
30 hold it on your lap. Never place it on the interviewer's desk.

Job Hunting Secrets

by KIRBY W. STANAT

Don't have unusually long fingernails. This applies to men as well as women. Really long fingernails could indicate that you haven't really worked in a
35 while—even office chores cause broken, and therefore shorter, fingernails.

Don't show your nervousness by drumming your fingers, swinging your leg, or cracking your knuckles. Men: don't have any loose change in your pocket—
40 most of us tend to jingle it when we are nervous. (You really shouldn't have your hands in your pockets in the first place.)

Don't keep adjusting your clothes.

Don't fiddle with your hair.
45 *Don't* compare this recruiter's office with others that you have seen. The recruiter might decide that you have seen the inside of too many employment offices, including his.

Don't pick up anything from the recruiter's desk
50 unless you are invited to do so.

Don't listen in on any phone calls the recruiter may receive while you are with him. Do your best to "tune out." After such a phone call, don't comment on something he said or ask a question about the
55 conversation.

Don't stand if someone else (man or woman) enters the recruiter's office. Keep your chair and don't say anything to the visitor unless you are spoken to first. If the recruiter introduces you to the person
60 who came in, then you can stand.

Don't inspect or read documents on the recruiter's desk.

Don't call the recruiter "sir" or "ma'am" too much. Respect is mandatory, but don't go overboard.
65 *Don't* overuse the interviewer's name . . . .

Don't be a jokester. Wisecracks and laughter can come later. Be pleasant, but remember that the interviewing process is formal and serious. An overly lighthearted approach will cause the interviewer to
70 question the seriousness of your purpose.

Don't give one- and two-word answers. The recruiter is trying to get to know you. Talk to him. If you go into a shell, you probably won't be hired.

Don't hog the conversation. Answer the questions
75 thoroughly, but don't drone on forever.

Don't interrupt. That's rude in a saloon, and it is inexcusable in an interviewing situation.

Don't use profanity, even if the recruiter does. It can't possibly help your image.
80 *Don't* use a lot of slang.

Don't gush. You can be pleasant without being syrupy.

Don't say "you know" all the time. It's, you know, annoying.
85 *Don't* call the interviewer by his or her first name.

Don't slip into a speech-making or preaching tone of voice. You're not on the Senate floor. You are in a conversation. Make sure you don't bellow.
90 *Don't* mumble.

Don't chatter while the interviewer is reviewing your resume. Let him read it in peace.

Don't interpret items on your resumé until you are asked. Your resumé should be self-explanatory. If additional details are needed, the interviewer will ask for them.

Don't try to overpower the recruiter with bragging or overstatement. He won't respond well, and he is probably skilled in recognizing distortions of background and experience.

Don't lie about anything. Sometimes candidates lie about their salary. Recruiters often ask for proof, such as a W-2 form.

Don't criticize your present employer too much. If it's a bad situation, you can mention it, but don't harp on it. You don't want to be considered a crank.

Don't ever get angry or even irritated during the interview. You can be firm—not angry—if the questioning becomes improper or begins to slip into irrelevant areas.

Don't answer questions that you don't want to answer because you consider them to be too personal—and explain your reasoning.

Don't look at your watch during the interview. This tends to hurry things along. Let the interviewer set the pace.

Don't ask, "Will I get the job?" or, "Can I have the job?" These questions tend to box the recruiter in and he won't like that. Rather say, "I hope you can consider me as a candidate for this job," or "I'm really interested in this job."

Don't talk about salary until later in the hiring process or until the interviewer brings it up.

DOS

Do make sure your hands are attractive. This means spotlessly clean with trimmed nails.

Do make sure that your hair is in place and conservative.

Do pay attention to your scent. Women with powerful perfumes and men with intense colognes can destroy interviews. Again, moderation is recommended.

Do go to the bathroom before you visit the employment lobby. It is embarrassing to interrupt an interview to "go," and you want to be as comfortable as possible during this "pressure cooker" happening.

Do get a good night's sleep before each day that you search for employment. If you yawn in the lobby or smother a yawn during the interview, it will cost you. Be rested and at your alert best.

Do look the interviewer in the eye. Recruiters place a lot of emphasis on eye contact.

Do try to sparkle. Use gestures in your conversation. Make sure they are smooth and emphatic.

Do smile.

Do make sure you get the interviewer's name right and use it a few times during the interview.

Do have some money with you. You never know what might happen. The interviewer might tell you he'd like you to take a cab to a consulting psychologist's office. You never want to be in the embarrassing position of having to say, "I don't have any money with me." The employer will almost always pay any expenses for something the company asks you to do . . . .

Do take notes if you wish. After all, the interviewer takes them. Why shouldn't you? You might consider writing down some questions before you go into the interview . . . .

Do let the interviewer set the pace of the interview. Let him lead with the questions.

Do let the interviewer decide when the interview is over.

Do ask the interviewer when you will hear from him again.

VOCABULARY LIST

secret *(n.)*   something kept from the knowledge of others; something known only to a few

forward *(adj.)*   on time; quick to act or respond

forward *(adj.)*   immodest; opposite of shy

fiddle *(v.)*   to make aimless movements with the hands

tune out *(two-word verb)*   not listen to

mandatory *(adj.)*   required

drone *(v.)*   to talk in a monotonous (without change in tone) voice

image *(n.)*   someone's idea of a person

slang *(n.)*   very informal speech, vivid and colorful

gush *(v.)*   to talk with a lot of enthusiasm, in a silly and emotional way

syrupy *(adj.)*   very sweet

bellow *(v.)*   to roar; shout

mumble *(v.)*   to speak indistinctly, as with partly closed lips

chatter *(v.)*   to talk rapidly, constantly, and pointlessly or foolishly

interpret *(v.)*   to explain the meaning of

brag *(v.)*   to boast; praise oneself

distortion *(n.)*   twisting or changing of the truth

criticize *(v.)*   to disapprove; find fault with

candidate *(n.)*   person who seeks a job or office

conservative *(adj.)*   traditional in style

moderation *(n.)*   freedom from excess (more than enough)

alert *(adj.)*   watchful; wide-awake

emphasis *(n.)*   importance

RESUMÉ

John Doe
1802 Berry Drive, N.E.
Atlanta, Georgia 30306
(404) 555-1111

EDUCATION: University of Georgia, Athens, Georgia, B.B.A., 1987.

Briarcliff High School, Atlanta, Georgia, 1983.

HONORS: University of Georgia: Magna Cum Laude, Dean's List.

Briarcliff High School: National Honor Society, Beta Club.

WORK EXPERIENCE: Accountant, John Brown Company, Atlanta, Georgia, 1987–1990.

Salesman during school vacations, Sandler Shoe Store, Atlanta, Georgia, 1982–1987.

PERSONAL DATA: Place of Birth: Atlanta, Georgia.
Date of Birth: February 23, 1965.

REFERENCES: Available upon request.

Activity: Presenting a Mock Job Interview

Several students volunteer to prepare mock job interviews for class presentation. The class offers appropriate criticism of "interviewers" and "applicants."

Reading Comprehension

TRUE/FALSE STATEMENTS

Answer the following statements True *or* False. *Try not to look back at the selection.*

_____ 1. Be a little ahead of time for an interview.

_____ 2. The interviewer will ask you to have a seat.

_____ 3. You don't want to have bad breath, so keep a mint in your mouth.

_____ 4. Wear your eyeglasses if you need them.

_____ 5. Put your handbag on the interviewer's desk so that no one will steal it.

_____ 6. Be sure to paint your long fingernails a pretty shade of red.

_____ 7. Men should keep their hands in their pockets unless their fingernails are clean.

_____ 8. Even though your hair looks terrible, don't comb it during an interview.

_____ 9. Show your respect by saying "sir" or "ma'am" from time to time.

_____ 10. Slang is more appropriate in casual conversation than in a formal situation like a job interview.

_____ 11. Call the interviewer by his first name so that he will think you like him.

_____ 12. It's not necessary to explain your resumé to the interviewer unless he asks you to.

_____ 13. Be sure to brag about yourself so that the interviewer will realize how much his company needs you.

_____ 14. Before the end of the interview, be sure to ask the interviewer if he has decided to hire you.

_____ 15. Smell sweet, but not so sweet that someone a mile away can smell you.

_____ 16. Keep your eye on the interviewer's desk at all times.

_____ 17. Don't smile, because a job interview is a very serious situation.

_____ 18. If the interviewer sends you to a psychologist, you can be sure you won't get the job.

_____ 19. You may take notes during an interview.

_____ 20. When you decide that the interview is over, leave.

Choose the correct answer for each of the following.

_____ 1. Your resumé would *not* include your
A. address.   C. education.
B. political beliefs.   D. work history.

_____ 2. A woman applying for a secretarial position would *not* wear one of the following to a job interview.
A. a jacket   C. a wristwatch
B. a diamond bracelet   D. a silk scarf

_____ 3. According to the reading selection, you should *always* take one of the following to a job interview.
A. a typewriter   C. your overcoat
B. an umbrella   D. money

_____ 4. If the interviewer receives a telephone call during the interview, you should
A. tune in.   C. tune off.
B. not listen.   D. leave the room.

_____ 5. It is better to "go"
A. during the interview.
B. in the taxi.
C. before the interview.
D. at the beginning of the interview.

_____ 6. Which one of the following questions would you consider too personal to answer?
A. Why did you leave your last job?
B. What was your salary on your last job?
C. What was your grade point average in college?
D. Do you have a boyfriend (girlfriend)?

Meaning from Context

Read the following excerpts from the reading selection. Try to guess the **meanings** of the <u>underlined</u> words, phrases, and idioms from their context.

_____ 1. "Don't wear your <u>outer clothes</u> into an interview. Take any kind of overcoat or topcoat off." (lines 6–7)
A. oldest clothes   C. overcoat and rubber boots
B. best clothes

_____ 2. "Don't show your nervousness by <u>drumming your fingers</u> . . . ." (lines 37–38)
   A. twisting your fingers
   B. tapping continuously on something with your fingers
   C. cracking the joints of your fingers

_____ 3. "Men: don't have any loose change in your pockets—most of us <u>tend</u> to jingle it when we are nervous." (lines 39–40)
   A. are likely   C. intend
   B. like

_____ 4. "Don't call the recruiter 'sir' or 'ma'am' too much. Respect is mandatory, but don't <u>go overboard</u>." (lines 63–64)
   A. throw yourself into the water
   B. overdo it   C. be impolite

_____ 5. "Don't give one- and two-word answers . . . . Talk to him. If you <u>go into a shell</u>, you probably won't be hired." (lines 71–73)
   A. become flustered   C. bellow
   B. are very shy

_____ 6. "Don't <u>hog the conversation</u>. Answer the questions thoroughly, but don't drone on forever." (lines 74–75)
   A. do all the talking   C. talk about irrelevant things
   B. talk about pigs

_____ 7. "Don't use <u>profanity</u> . . . ." (line 78)
   A. slang   C. curse words (violent and dirty
   B. bad grammar   language)

_____ 8. "Don't criticize your present employer too much. If it's a bad situation, you can mention it, but don't <u>harp on it</u>." (lines 104–106)
   A. find fault with it   C. lose your temper
   B. keep talking about it

_____ 9. "Do get a good night's sleep before each day that you search for employment . . . . Be rested and <u>at your alert best</u>." (lines 136–139)
   A. attentive   C. very polite
   B. look your best

_____ 10. "Do look the interviewer in the eye. Recruiters <u>place a lot of emphasis on eye contact</u>." (lines 140–141)
   A. prefer contact lenses to eyeglasses
   B. want you to have excellent vision
   C. want you to look directly at them

Idioms

SENTENCE COMPLETION

The following idioms include the word time. Study them carefully and then complete the following sentences using the appropriate idioms from the list. Each idiom will be used only once.

ahead of time early

all the time continuously; very often

for the time being for now

from time to time once in a while; occasionally

in no time in a very short time

in time early enough

in the nick of time (line 3) just at the right time; almost too late

on time at the specified time

take one's time not hurry

time after time again and again; repeatedly

1. All my friends volunteered to help me paint my apartment; we finished the job _____ .

2. I'm looking forward to your visit tonight. Try to come _____ to have dinner with me.

3. Mothers tell their children _____ not to cross the street without looking both ways.

4. If you want to see Michael Jackson perform, buy your concert tickets a month _____ .

5. Dentists work by appointment, and they expect their patients to be _____ .

6. Noriko wants to become a registered nurse. _____ , she is working as a nurse's aide.

7. You're walking much too fast. _____ !

8. The cookies almost burned; I took them out of the oven _____
_____.

9. Some children do not read well because they watch TV _____
_____.

10. We can't afford to eat out often, but we do go to a nice restaurant
_____.

Vocabulary

Write an original sentence using each of the following words.

1. lap: _____
_____
_____

2. elbow: _____
_____
_____

3. knuckles: _____
_____
_____

4. fingernails: _____
_____
_____

5. teeth: _____
_____
_____

What other parts of the body are mentioned in the selection?

Fill in the blanks in the following sentences with the appropriate words from the list below. Use correct verb tenses.

hog (v.)	lighthearted	salary
image	lobby	scent
interpret	mandatory	slang
interrupt	mumble	spotless
interviews	pace	wisecracks
irrelevant	recruiters	yawn
jingle	resumé	

1. When the famous actor visited Atlanta, Georgia, he refused to give any _____ to the press.

2. Marie and her husband sat in the _____ of the hotel for a while before they went up to their room.

3. Large companies send _____ to various colleges to hire bright young graduates.

4. Everyone enjoyed Mario's company because he was always making _____.

5. The bracelets on her arm _____ as she walked.

6. She was _____ that morning because she had done exceedingly well on her exams.

7. Drivers in the United States are supposed to stay in the right lane, but some of them like to _____ the road.

8. The expression "freak out" is considered _____.

9. The students asked the teacher to _____ the difficult passage in the reading selection.

10. A question about mathematics is _____ in an English class.

11. Four hundred dollars a week is a very good _____.

12. She scrubbed the kitchen floor until it was _____.

13. Roses have a lovely _____.

14. When people become bored or sleepy, they begin to _____.

15. If the President of the United States wore shorts and a torn T-shirt in the Oval Office (his office in the White House), his _____ would be destroyed!

16. No one was able to understand what he said because he _____ _____.

17. I had a hard time keeping up with him because he walked at a fast _____.

18. Please don't _____ me while I'm speaking.

19. It is _____ that every student in my class take the final exam.

20. A _____ does *not* include one's bank balance.

ANTONYMS

Choose the correct antonym from column (2) for each word in column (1). Use your English-English dictionary when necessary.

(1)	(2)
____ 1. prompt	A. fire
____ 2. forward	B. late
____ 3. erect	C. depressed
____ 4. nervousness	D. stooped
____ 5. pick up	E. dirty
____ 6. formal	F. bashful
____ 7. lighthearted	G. put down
____ 8. rude	H. ugly
____ 9. bellow	I. inattentive
____ 10. criticize	J. polite
____ 11. hire	K. casual
____ 12. attractive	L. calmness
____ 13. spotless	M. whisper
____ 14. alert	N. praise

Two very common suffixes in English are *-able* (sometimes *-ible*) and *-ness*.

Part 1

The suffix *-able* changes many **verbs** into **adjectives** and means "capable of being . . . ." For example: *manage + able = manageable* (capable of being managed).

Change each of the following **verbs** *into* **adjectives** *by adding* *-able. Then write a sentence with each new word. Follow the example. (Spelling Rule: Drop the final* **e** *before a suffix beginning with a vowel. Exception: The final* **e** *is retained after* **c** *or* **g** *when the suffix begins with* **a** *or* **o**.)

1. manage   <u>*manageable*</u>   (line 28)

   Everyone can manage a small car.

   <u>*A small car is manageable.*</u>

2. love   _____

   The whole world loves babies.

   _____

3. break   _____

   Be careful! Those dishes break easily.

   _____

4. notice   _____

   One can notice the scar on her face.

   _____

5. enjoy   _____

   We all enjoyed the party last night.

   _____

6. understand   _____

   I can always understand my teacher's lectures.

   _____

Part 2

The suffix -ness changes many **adjectives** into **nouns** and means "quality or state of being . . . ." For example: nervous + ness = nervousness (state of being nervous).

Change each of the following **adjectives** *into* **nouns** *by adding* **-ness.** *Then write a sentence with each new word. Follow the example. (Spelling Rule: In words ending in* **y** *preceded by a consonant, change* **y** *to* **i** *before any suffix except one beginning with* **i.**)

1. nervous   <u>*nervousness*</u>   (line 37)

   He was nervous when he took the test.

   <u>*His nervousness was obvious when he took the test.*</u>

2. kind   _____

   She was kind to her friends in many ways.

   _____

3. lazy   _____

   He didn't make good grades because he was lazy.

   _____

4. blind   _____

   Allen went to school even though he was blind.

   _____

5. sad   _____

   I could see that her eyes were sad.

   _____

Richard Reeves, syndicated columnist, writes: "In this smaller world, you have to know English to 'keep up' with modern developments . . . ." Yet many countries want to stop the spread of English. Why? Mr. Reeves answers this question in his column.

"The mushroom growth of English medium schools should be checked, as they will be a source of trouble . . . ." That was the warning last month in Lahore, Pakistan, in a Pakistan Times article on the problems of illiteracy in the country and the fact that more and more Pakistanis would rather be literate in English than in Urdu, the country's official language.

It is pretty much the same almost everywhere in the world. Almost 800 million people now speak English as a first or second language—an increase of about 40 percent in the past twenty years. The language of the British and the Americans—American English is now the driving force—has become the language of communication among national elites, the language of people who want to "get ahead," the language of technology, science, trade, diplomacy and of an internationalizing popular culture.

In this smaller world, you have to know English to "keep up" with modern developments—something like 80 percent of the world's technical papers are first published in English. If you want to know—now!—what is happening in computers or aviation, in accounting or rock music, you have to know English.

That's why 117 million foreigners—non-residents of the 37 countries where English is an official language—are studying the language now. According to the United Nations Statistical Yearbook, 16 percent of the primary-school students are studying the language. In the Arabic-speaking countries, science and mathematics courses are taught in English.

In the Soviet Union, more than half the country's high-school students are studying English—and most of them seem to stop American visitors on the street

American English: A World Language

by RICHARD REEVES

been some successes in reducing the use of the language—in Vietnam and Iran, for example.

But there is only so far a country can go in denying the language of modernity. U Ne Win, the ruler of Burma, forbade English instruction in his country for years—until his own daughter was refused admission to British medical schools because of an English-language deficiency. Now, English is a mandatory subject in Burma from kindergarten through college.

All of that, obviously, means a lot more to Americans than just making it easier to travel almost anywhere these days. There has not been a great deal of study done about the cultural, social and political impact and implications of the "mushroom" spread of a language—this is a new situation—but if "the medium is the message" and the medium is our language, then it may follow that the message that gets through will be our message.

THE FAMILY CIRCUS   **by Bill Keane**

11-24
Copyright 1987
Cowles Syndicate, Inc.

"Why do I have to keep writin' in these K's when they don't make any noise anyway?"

to practice the language. The same thing happens again and again to Americans in China.

And people, in Pakistan and other places, are learning it on their own, to get ahead. So, Pakistan is worried about preserving its own language and culture—the country's leaders worry that American ideas and habits are traveling with American words.

There has never been a world language to match modern English. Latin in its time, Italian in the 16th and 17th centuries and French in the 18th and 19th centuries did not come close to the penetration and pervasiveness of English today. Or the growth—it seems likely that by the year 2000 there will be more non-native English speakers than native.

Much of the world would like to stop that spread. There are anti-English programs in the Philippines and Taiwan and other unlikely places. There have

VOCABULARY LIST

source *(n.)* place or thing from which something comes

warning *(n.)* notice that something harmful or bad is going to happen

official (ə <u>fish</u> əl) *(adj.)* authorized or approved by a government

elite *(n.)* the most powerful or most intelligent persons in a group; persons of the highest class

diplomacy *(n.)* conduct by government officials of negotiations and other relations between nations

primary school *(n.)* first three or four grades of the elementary school

preserve *(v.)* to keep unchanged; to protect

penetration *(n.)* act of entering and spreading

pervasiveness *(n.)* act of spreading throughout

reduce *(v.)* to make smaller

deficiency (di <u>fish</u> ənsi) *(n.)* lack or absence of something needed or required

impact *(n.)* influence; the effect of one thing upon another

Reading Comprehension

TRUE/FALSE STATEMENTS

Answer the following statements True or False.

_____ 1. An increasing number of Pakistanis would rather be illiterate in Urdu than in English.

_____ 2. Forty percent of the people in the world have begun to speak English in the past twenty years.

_____ 3. British English rather than American English is preferred among the most intelligent people in the world.

_____ 4. The majority of the world's technical papers are first published in English.

_____ 5. Over fifty percent of the high-school students in Russia study English.

_____ 6. The reader can infer that English is not taught in the schools in China.

_____ 7. According to Richard Reeves, ambitious people in Pakistan and other countries are teaching themselves English.

_____ 8. French, at one time, was as popular a language in the world as English is today.

_____ 9. By the twenty-first century, there will be fewer native speakers of English than non-native speakers.

_____ 10. English has always been a required language in the schools in Burma.

Meaning from Context

MULTIPLE CHOICE

*Read the following excerpts from the reading selection. Choose the appropriate **meaning** for each underlined part of the sentences. Use the **context**—what comes before and after a word, phrase, sentence, etc.—to help you choose the correct meaning.*

_____ 1. "'The mushroom growth of English medium schools should be checked, as they will be a source of trouble . . . .'" (lines 1–3)

A. The vast number of average English schools should be discouraged.

B. The rapid increase of schools in which subjects are taught in English should be stopped.

C. The increasing number of English middle schools should be ignored.

(*Hint:* Look up the various meanings of "medium" in your English-English dictionary.)

_____ 2. "The language of the British and the Americans . . . has become the language of communication among national elites, the language of people who want to 'get ahead' . . . ." (lines 11–15)

A. be successful

B. travel

C. earn a living

_____ 3. "In this smaller world, you have to know English to 'keep up' with modern developments—something like 80 percent of the world's technical papers are first published in English." (lines 18–21)

A. be intelligent

B. stay up-to-date

C. communicate with young people

What do you *think* the <u>underlined</u> portions of the following excerpts mean? Study the **context.**

1. "So, Pakistan is worried about preserving its own language and culture—the country's leaders worry that <u>American ideas and habits are traveling with American words.</u>" (lines 38–41)

2. "There has not been a great deal of study done about the cultural, social and political impact and implications of the 'mushroom' spread of a language . . . but if 'the medium is the message' and the medium is our language,* then it may follow that <u>the message that gets through will be our message.</u>" (lines 63–69)
   (*Hint:* Do *mushrooms* multiply rapidly? What does "medium" mean in this context?)

Vocabulary

ORAL EXERCISE

Answer the following questions.

1. Do you think the increase in drug use has had an *impact* on the crime rate? Explain your answer.
2. What do you think can be done to *reduce* the number of auto accidents?
3. How old were you when you were in *primary school?*
4. Who do you think would head the list of the *elite* in British society?
5. What *warning* would you give a friend who was smoking two packages of cigarettes a day?
6. Name some *sources* of air pollution. Of water pollution.
7. What is the *official* language of your country? Does the United States have an official language?
8. What beverage would you drink to help correct a calcium *deficiency?*
9. According to Richard Reeves, what are some countries doing to *preserve* their own cultures?

---

* *our language:* American English

Part 1

You have learned that the noun suffix -*ness* changes **adjectives** into **nouns.** The noun suffix -*ion* (-*ation, -sion*) changes **verbs** into **nouns** and means "act of; condition." For example: *communication* means *act of communicating* (line 14).

Change the **verbs** *listed below into* **nouns** *by adding the suffix* **-ion** *(-ation, -sion). Write sentences using the verbs in the list and the nouns you have formed. Use your English-English dictionary when necessary. Follow the example. (Spelling Rule: The silent* **e** *is dropped before a suffix beginning with a vowel. Note: Some verbs alter their spelling when the suffix is added.)*

1. protect ___*The Secret Service protects the U.S. President.*___

   (n.) ___*protection*___

   ___*The Secret Service provides protection for the U.S. President.*___

2. decide _____

   _____

   (n.) _____

   _____

   _____

3. retaliate _____

   _____

   (n.) _____

   _____

   _____

4. adopt _____

   _____

   (n.) _____

   _____

   _____

5. graduate _____

   _____

   (n.) _____

   _____

   _____

6. explain _____

   _____

   (n.) _____

   _____

   _____

Part 2

The suffixes *-er/-ar/-or/-ist* indicate **nouns** and mean "one who" or "that which." For example: *gunner* (line 10, Chapter 5) means a sailor who fires a gun.

Circle the **noun suffix** *in each of the words below. (Note that the final* **e** *is dropped from the* **base** *word when the suffix begins with a vowel.) Then write the definition of each noun. Follow the example.*

act(or): *A person who acts in stage plays, movies, etc.*

washer: *A large appliance that washes clothes*

liar: _____

typist: _____

visitor: _____

guitarist: _____

adviser: _____

tourist: _____

toaster: _____

racist: _____

About 55.9% of women over 16 in the United States work outside the home; 52% of American women whose children are under 3 are in the work force. These women are having to face the same "problem" that columnist Ellen Goodman found was troubling Soviet women who worked outside the home. (Ms. Goodman visited Russia in 1985.) In her column, "The Soviet Superwoman," she believes "the problem is universal and unresolved." Ellen Goodman writes about a range of contemporary issues.

MOSCOW — Eventually it comes up in any conversation with Soviet women. They don't call it the Superwoman Syndrome here. It is simply the Problem of Women: the double burden of work and fam-
5 ily.

The first time the subject arises is in an official meeting with the Soviet Women's Committee: "There are some traditions which are dying very slowly," says Xenia Proskurnikova, the first vice-president,
10 "especially the idea that housework is only a woman's occupation." When I ask if any of the prominent women around the table has a husband who shares the housework equally, there is an awkward, smiling silence.

15 The next time is in a private gathering when a young university professor says: "We have two problems, queues [the shopping lines] and men.

The Soviet Superwoman

by ELLEN GOODMAN

I think we will solve the problem of queues before
we solve the problem of men." A third time is in an
interview with sociologists who add another familiar
dimension to the problem: the inflexibility of the
work world.

In some ways it is remarkably easy to talk here
about the Problem of Women. The dialogue cuts
through politics and rhetoric, to everyday dilemmas
familiar to women in both the U.S. and Soviet cultures. In another way it is unsettling, precisely because the problem is universal, and unresolved. Neither of these two vastly different systems has figured
out a way to balance the demands of work and family;
neither has distributed the private work load fairly
between men and women.

More than half the workers in the Soviet Union
are women. More than 90 percent of adult women
are either workers or students. Nevertheless, romanticism and chauvinism run deep.

The same people who talk practically about
women as comrades turn sentimental talking about
motherhood. Zoya Krylova, the enthusiastic forty-
year-old editor of *Working Woman,* is typical . . . .
Her magazine serves as a gutsy advocate for the rights
of its 16 million female readers at the workplace.

Yet, she says, "We are also trying to teach a woman
to stay a woman in the family. Women are the heart
of the family and must be warmer to create the at-
mosphere of warmth and love." . . .

The research on young women shows, not sur-
prisingly, that they want a marriage in which husband
and wife are equals, but the reality is, also not sur-
prisingly, different. The Soviet versions of "the new
man" are few and nurtured hopefully by women.
When one such man wrote into the paper about how
his co-workers heckled him for sharing duties with
his wife, 5,000 women wrote in his support.

But many men, perhaps most, simply resist taking
on "women's work." Some of the most contemporary
husbands speak with the edge of smugness in the
voice of this thirty-year-old husband: "Women have
learned it's hard to make a career at the office and so
nerve-wracking that they don't really want it." His
wife translated this, dissenting all the way. A more
moderate, chivalrous chauvinism was echoed by so-
ciologist Vladimir Lisovski: "First of all a man should
be more responsible for his family. But with all due
respect to the emancipation of women, I'm convinced
men should be the head of the family."

A number of women complain in turn that since
the postwar years, when Russian men were an endangered species, the men have been pampered beyond redemption. As one twenty-year-old student
said in words much harsher than her gentle voice, "I
want to say that the boys of my age are so spoiled by
their mothers that they never help in the family life."
An older, divorced journalist said, "I had the choice
of doing all the work without complaint, or fighting
all the time, or getting divorced." The Soviet Union
has a divorce rate that matches our own, and 70
percent of divorces are initiated by women. More

than a few of these marriages falter on these 80 "choices."

Of course, the Problem of Women is not without its problem solvers. In the big cities now, some workplaces have food concessions to cut down on shopping. The government is increasing child care as the 85 web of grandmothers breaks down. In a few schools, boys are being taught to cook along with girls.

But the biggest policy push is not directed at men or institutions, but at the clock. The latest plans call for more flexible work hours for mothers; the latest 90 hopes are for more part-time work. Eugenia Zubareva, who runs the social welfare system for the city of Leningrad, says that if Mikhail Gorbachev came to her office, "I would ask him to make women less engaged at work so they could spend more time with 95 their children." It is a sentiment that I hear echoed again and again.

It is hard to compare the lives of Soviet and American women. The Soviet officials boast of paid maternity leave and child care centers; the Americans 100 boast of supermarkets, cars, and washing machines.

But in any circle of working mothers, the word *time* resonates across cultures. Women have been in the work force a generation longer here and the "problem" is just as acute. It is basically women who 105 are spreading their energy thinly across all needs. Maybe this is what happens anywhere that balancing work and family is still called "the Problem of Women." MAY 1985

"SUPERMOM"   **by David Wink**

VOCABULARY LIST

syndrome *(n.)*   characteristic pattern of behavior

awkward *(adj.)*   embarrassing

dialogue *(n.)*   conversation

rhetoric *(n.)*   use of exaggeration in language to impress others

dilemma *(n.)*   difficult choice to be made between two courses of action

unsettling *(adj.)*   disturbing

romanticism *(n.)*   characteristic of being sentimental, emotional rather than practical

chauvinism *(n.)*   belief that one's own sex is superior to the other

gutsy *(adj.)* *(slang)*   courageous

advocate *(n.)*   person who supports an idea

nurture *(v.)*   to support and encourage

heckle *(v.)*   to annoy and embarrass by making unfriendly remarks

smugness *(n.)*   being too pleased or satisfied with oneself

dissent *(v.)*   to differ in opinion

chivalrous *(adj.)*   courteous, especially toward women

emancipation *(n.)*   social and political freedom

endangered species *(adj.; n.)*   class of individuals small and decreasing in number

pamper *(v.)*   to spoil

initiate *(v.)*   to start

acute *(adj.)*   severe, serious

Reading Comprehension

QUESTIONS AND DISCUSSION

Answer the following questions.

1. When Ellen Goodman visited Russia in 1985, she found it "remarkably easy to talk here about the Problem of Women." Explain in your own words "the Problem of Women."

2. "They don't call it the Superwoman Syndrome here. It is simply the Problem of Women . . . ." How do these statements imply that women in the Soviet Union and the United States face the same problem? (*Hint:* Where is *here?*) Define "superwoman" in the context of this article.

3. The author quotes a university professor: " 'We have two problems, queues [the shopping lines] and men. I think we will solve the problem of queues before we solve the problem of men.' " Explain "the problem of men." Underline all portions of the article that you think refer to "the problem of men."

4. Since World War II, why have Russian men been spoiled by their mothers? Are men in your culture pampered by their mothers? If so, give some examples of how they are pampered.

5. According to Ms. Goodman, what was being done in Russia to help women who were in the work force?

6. Explain: "But in any circle of working mothers, the word *time* resonates [is heard loudly] across cultures." Do you have "the Problem of Women" in your country? Why or why not? Are men in your culture chauvinistic? Explain your answer.

TRUE/FALSE STATEMENTS

Answer the following statements True *or* False. *If the statement is false,* explain why *in the space provided.*

_____ 1. In 1985, about 90% of the workers in Russia were women.

_____

_____ 2. The modern Soviet woman still wants to remain the center of her family.

_____

_____ 3. In Russia, male chauvinism is a thing of the past.

_____

———————— 4. In 1985, the rate of divorce in Russia was the same as in the United States.

———————————————————

———————— 5. The majority of divorces in Russia are begun by men who think their wives should be simply housewives.

———————————————————

———————— 6. This article implies that in the past grandmothers babysat while mothers worked outside the home.

———————————————————

———————— 7. Russian women who become pregnant are fired from their jobs.

———————————————————

———————— 8. Women in the Soviet Union have been in the work place about 30 years longer than women in the United States.

Vocabulary

ORAL EXERCISE

Answer the following questions.

1. Are you an *advocate* of abortion? Why or why not?
2. Do you think asking a woman her age is a universally *awkward* question? Explain your answer.
3. How does the word *emancipation* apply to the people of the East European countries?
4. How should a speaker react if someone in the audience *heckles* him/her?
5. Are men in your country *chivalrous*? Do you think American men are *chivalrous*? Explain your answer.
6. Is it a good idea to have a *dialogue* with your enemy? Why or why not?
7. What is an antonym for *gutsy*?
8. Why do you think a large number of students *dissented* when their teacher decided to give no tests during the quarter, only a final exam?
9. Anna needed to work to help support her family. Yet she was afraid a day care center would not give her baby the best of care. Anna was in a ————————. (Complete the sentence with the appropriate word from the Vocabulary List on page 101.)

TWO-WORD VERBS

The verb *come,* when combined with certain particles, changes its meaning. For example: to *come up* (line 1) means to *be introduced into a conversation.*

Read the following conversation aloud with a partner. Then <u>underline</u> the phrasal verbs with **come** *and try to guess their meanings.*

FRED: Come in, Jim. The door's unlocked.

JIM: Hi, Fred. The movie starts in half an hour. Come on, or we'll be late.

FRED: We have time. Here's an article I came across in yesterday's paper. I think you'll find it interesting.

JIM: Thanks. By the way, how did the game come out last night?

FRED: The Braves lost. We've had bad luck this season, but maybe the team will come through tonight.

JIM: By the way, I've got a couple of pizzas in my freezer. How about coming over after the movie.

FRED: Sounds good! It's getting late. Let's go.

Note: The phrasal verbs that you underlined are all *inseparable.*

Review

Phrasal Verbs

SENTENCE COMPLETION

*Fill in each blank in the following sentences with the appropriate phrasal verb from the list below. Use **correct verb tenses.***

break down	*get away with*	*look for*
break into	*get on*	*look like*
break out	*get out of*	*look over*
break up	*get over*	*look up*
count off	*get through*	*make up*
find out	*go with*	*pick up*
get along	*look after*	

1. My neighbor is going to _____ my cat while I'm out of town.

2. John quit his job because he couldn't _____ with his boss.

3. The psychologist helped the little boy _____ his fear of the dark.

4. Gilmar and his girl friend _____ when he _____ _____ she had dated another boy.

5. Gilmar and his girl friend kissed and _____ after she promised she would date only Gilmar!

6. My car _____ yesterday. Would you please _____ me _____ on your way to school?

7. When Maribel _____ taking her final exam, she _____ it _____ carefully and then handed it in.

8. Jose _____ the meanings of unfamiliar words in his English-English dictionary.

9. Helen and Jimmy _____ each other for two years before they got married.

10. Abby and her twin sister Ann _____ each other.

11. Three fire engines arrived five minutes after the fire _____ _____.

12. _____ the bus in front of the park.

13. Someone _____ my car and stole my new coat.

14. Can't you _____ going to the meeting? There's a great movie playing at the Lenox Square theater.

15. How many years did Harriet Magnis _____ lying to her husband?

16. Wei Shin _____ his eyeglasses for fifteen minutes before he realized they were parked on top of his head.

17. The instructions at the beginning of this test imply that Mrs. Cohen will _____ for incorrect verb tenses.

BEETLE BAILEY   **by Mort Walker**

Some of the following statements make little sense because they contain the **wrong** *phrasal verbs. Rewrite any such statements, and use the* **appropriate** *phrasal verbs.*

1. I certainly want to come to your birthday party. Count me out!

   _____

   _____

2. Pablo parked his car in the parking lot and got off.

   _____

   _____

3. Our teacher told us to make up ten good questions about the reading selection.

   _____

   _____

4. Tieng ran over a bus and wrecked his car.

   _____

   _____

5. The police broke up the noisy party at midnight.

   _____

   _____

6. I know you're very busy, but can you get away next week-end? I'd like you to go to the beach with me.

   _____

   _____

7. Martha gets off reading class at 12:50.

   _____

8. Always look after your homework so that you can correct any mistakes before you hand it in.

   _____

   _____

Write an original sentence using each of the following phrasal verbs.

1. look forward to: _____

_____

2. look up to: _____

_____

3. run out of: _____

_____

4. come out: _____

_____

5. go with (someone): _____

_____

Activity: Vocabulary Bee

You will enter a contest—a **vocabulary bee. A bee** is a gathering where people compete. You and your classmates will take turns defining, or making a sentence with, the words and idioms you have studied so far in this book. Your teacher will explain the rules of the contest. Prizes will be given to the champions!

PART TWO

Art Buchwald explains in his usual humorous fashion why foreigners often misinterpret what Americans say.

WASHINGTON — The trouble with foreigners in this country is that they take everything Americans say literally. I have a French friend named Michel. I met him the other day on the street, and after the
5 usual <u>chitchat</u>, I said, "Give me a call some time."

The next day he was on the line.

"*Bonjour*," he said, "It's Michel. You said to give you a call."

"I did?"

10 "*Oui*, don't you remember? I spoke to you yesterday on Pennsylvania Avenue."

"I didn't mean to call right away. It was just a nice way to say goodbye."

"Then you don't want to talk on the telephone?"

15 "I can't think of anything to say, frankly."

"But you asked me to call you."

Don't Say 'Let's Get Together' to a Foreigner

by ART BUCHWALD

"Look, I'm terribly busy right now. Let's have lunch some time."

"I would like that. When?"

20 "I'm not sure. Why don't you give me a holler?"

Two days later I heard someone calling my name from the sidewalk. I opened the window in my office and Michel was down below.

"What in the devil are you shouting about?" I 25 yelled down to him.

"You said give you a holler when I wanted to have lunch. How about today?"

"I'm busy today."

"Why did you tell me to give you a holler when I 30 wanted to have lunch if you were so tied up?"

"When an American says, 'Let's have lunch some time,' he doesn't necessarily mean it. It's a pleasantry.

You French say, 'Au revoir,' the Germans say, 'Auf wiedersehen,' the Spanish say 'Hasta manana,' and 35 Americans say, 'Let's have lunch,' which in our country means, 'Don't call me, I'll call you.' "

Michel said, "I didn't mean to bother you."

"You didn't bother me. I'll tell you what. Let's check in with each other and have a drink one of 40 these days."

"That would be great," Michel said.

I was sweating out a column the next day when Michel stuck his head in.

"Now what?"

45 "I'm just checking in to see if you wanted a drink."

"Can't you see I'm busy?"

"I can see that now, but I couldn't before I checked in with you."

"You're driving me nuts. The only reason I said 50 'Let's have a drink some time' is because I wanted you to stop hollering under my window."

"All you have to do is tell me you don't want to see me," Michel said in a hurt voice, "instead of asking me to meet with you and breaking the date."

55 I felt badly. "You're right. I feel terrible about the way I've treated you. We're so used to saying goodbye to each other with a promise to get together soon, that no one in America expects the other person to keep it. We wouldn't get anything done if we had 60 lunch with everyone we met on the street."

"I understand," Michel said. "But if you change your mind, you have my card and you can call me."

"I don't have your card, Michel. That's another thing you don't understand. When Americans ex- 65 change business cards with each other, they usually throw them away when they get home."

Reading Comprehension

Answer the following questions.

1. According to Mr. Buchwald, why do foreigners often misinterpret what Americans say? What does *literal* mean?
2. What does "Let's get together" mean to a foreigner? What does it sometimes mean to the American who says it? Michel took "Give me a holler" literally. Explain.
3. What are some pleasantries that Americans use to end a conversation? What are some pleasantries that people use to end a conversation in your country?
4. Why do you think Americans exchange business cards and then later throw them away?
5. Have you ever had an experience similar to Michel's in Mr. Buchwald's column? Why do you think "Have a good day" annoys some Americans?

Vocabulary

MEANING FROM CONTEXT

This chapter and the remaining chapters in the book do *not* contain *vocabulary lists.* You will try to guess the meanings of words and phrases from their **context**—what comes before and after a word, phrase, or sentence to help you guess the meaning.

Read the sentences below. Try to guess the meaning of each underlined expression from its context. (These expressions are also underlined in the reading selection.) The **boldface** *words and phrases will help you.*

1. Bill wished his friends wouldn't **talk** to him while he was studying. He didn't have time for chitchat.

   chitchat: _____

2. If you **need help** when you move into your apartment, just give me a holler.

   give me a holler: _____

3. Every time I telephone my friend, her mother says she's <u>tied up</u> and **can't come to the phone.**

   tied up: _____

4. Jane's grandfather was very old and lived alone. **Every morning** Jane <u>checked in</u> with him to **ask how he felt** and **if he needed anything.**

   checked in: _____

5. Sara spent three days writing an essay for her writing class. Then she had to <u>sweat out</u> the **many revisions** (corrections and improvements) that her teacher suggested.

   sweat out: _____

6. A **dripping faucet** can <u>drive a person nuts</u>!
   People **who talk during a movie** <u>drive me nuts</u>!

   drive someone nuts: _____

7. My boy friend was going to **take me out** to eat last night. He had to <u>break the date</u> because he **got sick.**

   break a date: _____

DENNIS THE MENACE
by Hank Ketcham

"COULD YOU CALL BACK LATER? SHE'S ON ANOTHER LINE."

When the Carter Presidential Center in Atlanta, Georgia, was opened to the public in
October, 1986, there was a ceremony—a
dedication—to mark the occasion. President
Reagan came from Washington to give the
principal address, in which he spoke very
highly of former President Carter. The following is an excerpt from President Reagan's
speech.

Going through the Jimmy Carter Library just now,
and admiring the many photographs and films,* it
struck me that perhaps the central gift that this center
will give to the nation is a story. A story of one man's
5   life. A story that is distinctively American.

In one of its aspects, the story of President Carter
is the story of the family in which he grew up. Jimmy
Carter's father taught him the virtues of hard work
and self-discipline.

10   From the time he was 6, he knew that when the
farm bell rang, James Earl Sr. expected to see him
out of bed and going to work with everybody else.
He and his sisters and brother, Gloria, Ruth and Billy,
gave each other strength and support. Ruth, espe-

---

* The Carter Library and Museum houses 27 million
pages of presidential documents and thousands of pictures.

Dedication of the Carter Presidential Library

by RONALD REAGAN

15 cially, providing counsel through all the long years, all the joys and disappointments until her death in 1983.

He misses her still, as do all that knew her.

And then there was Miss Lillian, exuberant Miss 20 Lillian. Miss Lillian who went to work for the Peace Corps in India at the age of 69. Miss Lillian taught Jimmy Carter charity and justice. She taught him to care for all, regardless of race, especially those weaker and less fortunate than himself. And she taught him 25 to laugh.

Surely, Mr. President, James Earl Sr., Ruth and your precious mother, Miss Lillian, are with us today as we dedicate this center in honor of one whom they loved so much.

30 In another of its important aspects, the story of President Carter is the story of the South. For when Jimmy Carter was born on this date in 1924, many Southerners knew only poverty, and millions lived lives that were separate and unequal because of the 35 color of their skin.

There's a photograph inside the library that sets the scene. A little boy is drinking from a fountain. He's black. He's drinking from that particular fountain because on a tree next to the fountain, there's a 40 sign that reads "colored."

Well, the world has changed now. It has changed because men and women like Jimmy Carter stood up in church to protest the exclusion of black people from worship. And it has changed because Jimmy 45 Carter spoke those words in his inauguration address as governor of Georgia. Quote, "I say to you quite frankly that the time for racial discrimination is over. No poor, rural, weak or black person should ever again have to bear the additional burden of being 50 deprived of an opportunity for an education, a job or simple justice."

That old world has been replaced by a New South. A South that combines the best regional traditions of pride and hospitality with a new sense of openness 55 and opportunity for all. For at the same time they were combating discrimination, Southerners like Jimmy Carter were hard at work applying new techniques to farming, opening new businesses and encouraging new industry. And in so doing, they were 60 expanding economic opportunity and raising levels of education at historic rates.

One need only to look at Atlanta, bustling, prosperous Atlanta, to see that the South has truly risen again—transformed, self-confident, moving vigor- 65 ously on to still greater justice and opportunity.

So, in dedicating this center today, I want to express what all of us feel today in this beautiful Georgia landscape—that this celebration is in a sense a celebration of the South, the new South that Jimmy 70 Carter helped to build.

Reading Comprehension

Answer the following questions.

1. President Carter wrote about his mother in his autobiography. President Reagan spoke about her at the dedication of the Carter Library. What kind of person do you think Lillian Carter was? Write a short paragraph describing her.
2. What do you think Jimmy Carter learned from his parents that helped him become the leader of a great nation?
3. "... millions lived lives that were separate and unequal because of the color of their skin." What does President Reagan mean by this? Does he give an example? If so, what?
4. President Reagan says "the world has changed now." What does this mean and do you agree? If you disagree, why?
5. President Reagan talks about the "New South." In what ways does he say the South has changed?

Vocabulary

Read the following excerpts from the reading selection. The words and phrases that are underlined once will help you guess the meanings of the words that are underlined twice.

1. "Jimmy Carter's father taught him the virtues of hard work and self-discipline." (lines 7–9)

   virtues: _____

   (*Hint:* Are hard work and self-discipline good qualities?)

2. "Miss Lillian taught Jimmy Carter charity and justice. She taught him to care for all, regardless of race, especially those weaker and less fortunate than himself." (lines 21–24)

   charity: _____

   justice: _____

3. "He's <u>drinking</u> from that particular <u>fountain</u> . . . ." (lines 38–39)

fountain: _____

4. "It [the world] has changed because <u>men and women like Jimmy Carter stood up in church</u> to <u>protest</u> the <u>exclusion</u> of <u>black people</u> from <u>worship</u>." (lines 41–44)

protest: _____

exclusion: _____

worship: _____

5. "<u>No poor, rural, weak or black person</u> should ever again have to bear the additional burden of being <u>deprived</u> of an <u>opportunity</u> for an <u>education, a job or simple justice</u>." (lines 48–51)

deprived: _____

6. "One need only to look at Atlanta, <u>bustling</u>, <u>prosperous</u> Atlanta . . . ." (lines 62–63)

bustling: _____

(*Hint:* Is a large, prosperous city a center of activity?)

At least 20–30 million adults in the United States are functionally illiterate; that is, they are unable to read, write, or compute well enough to hold a job or meet the needs of everyday living. The literacy programs now in existence reach only a small percentage of the illiterate population. However, a growing awareness and concern about this problem have made the advancement of literacy a high priority issue for politicians, business-people, and ordinary American citizens.

In this selection, Chet Fuller, columnist for The Atlanta Constitution, *writes a sad story of a man afflicted with "the condition."*

It was an ordinary event, one that surely must be repeated dozens of times a day. In supermarkets, restaurants, movie theaters, department stores and office buildings across the nation. Still, it caught me
5 unawares.

Not that I'm unfamiliar with the condition. I write about it often, in editorials, in columns. I even know, personally, a few people who suffer from it.

But, it is not something I confront every day as I
10 travel the circles that make up my life. People who have the condition often are adept at hiding it. They resort to elaborate means to cover it up. That's understandable, since there is still a large stigma attached to it.

15 I would have never suspected the man who stood next to me in the supermarket the other day of being

He Was as Easy for Me to Read as the Pages of an Open Book

by CHET FULLER

afflicted. He seemed so confident, so self-assured. That is, until he kept staring at, first, the grocery list in his hand, then the items on the shelf in front of us.

He was tall and slender. His clothes were a working man's clothes. The veins that stood out on his muscular arms let me know he was used to hard work. I figured his wife had sent him to pick up a few things.

"Excuse me," he said softly. "Is this vanilla flavoring?" He was holding a small, yellow box he'd picked up from a shelf that contained hundreds of brightly colored boxes, bottles and cans of herbs and spices. There was a puzzled look on his face.

"It says *imitation* vanilla flavoring," I said. "That's real vanilla extract over there." His eyes stared in the direction I had pointed. He slid his cap back on his head. He really seemed confused now. A woman who had come up behind us tried to help: "The imitation's just as good, and it's cheaper," she said, nodding her head.

"Thank you," he said, putting the box of flavoring in his cart. At that moment, it dawned on me what was happening. *The poor guy couldn't read.* He had the condition.

A terrible sadness swept over me. That's why he had waited until there were only two of us standing in front of the spice shelves. He didn't want other people to hear him ask if he'd picked up the right item.

I started to move on, then stopped. He was still pondering his list and looking at the spices on the shelf, trying to match the writing on the list with the writing on the packages he saw. That way, he hoped to make the right choices. I felt sorry for him.

I went back to the shelf and pretended to be looking for a spice I couldn't find. I called out the names of the ones I saw and asked myself aloud did I need this one or that one. He listened. Soon, he picked up another box, smiled and said: "Thanks, Bro." Then he pushed his cart down the aisle.

I ran into him several times after that, on other aisles. He would stand for awhile comparing his list to the names of the items on the shelves. When he made a selection, he seemed so unsure. His cart was filling up awfully slowly. I could imagine his frustration.

I started to confront him, pull him aside and tell him that, if reading were his problem, I knew of places where he could get help. I even thought of offering to tutor him myself.

But I didn't do it. I didn't want to embarrass him, and I was afraid. I kept thinking it wouldn't be appropriate, somehow, for me to confront him over his inability to read. I did not want him to think I felt superior or benevolent. I did not want to challenge his manhood or self-esteem.

But I knew the wonderful new world that being able to read would open up to him. It would surely

119

make his life less complicated. He wouldn't have to pretend any more.

Here he was one of the real, flesh-and-blood people behind the statistics you hear about so much: that 80 more than a fourth of all adults in this country are functionally illiterate.

I didn't help him. I failed. And I still don't really know why.

Reading Comprehension

TRUE/FALSE STATEMENTS

Answer each of the following statements True *or* False *and give the reason for your answer.*

_____ 1. Since Mr. Fuller is obviously a well-educated man, he had never had the opportunity to meet an illiterate person before the incident in the supermarket.

_____ 2. What the writer witnessed in the supermarket is not an uncommon occurrence in the United States.

_____ 3. One can easily detect (discover) if a person is illiterate.

_____ 4. The reader can infer from Mr. Fuller's column that one is never too old to learn to read.

_____ 5. People who are illiterate are necessarily unintelligent. (Use your own judgment in answering this.)

_____ 6. More than 25% of all adults in the United States are not able to read and write at all.

QUESTIONS AND DISCUSSION

Answer the following questions.

1. Briefly, and in your own words, what is this reading selection about? What do you think the writer's purpose was in writing this column?
2. How does Mr. Fuller hold his readers in suspense? What does "the condition" mean?
3. What does the writer infer (conclude) from the man's physical appearance?
4. Why do you think the illiterate man addressed the writer as "Bro"?

5. Do you think the writer is a compassionate person? Explain why or why not. Why is Chet Fuller disappointed in himself?
6. Why is the title of the reading selection appropriate to the column?
7. Many prison inmates are illiterate. Do you think there is a connection between illiteracy and crime? Explain your answer.
8. Do you have an illiteracy problem in your country? If so, what is being done about it?

Vocabulary

MEANING FROM CONTEXT

Read the following excerpts from the selection. Circle the correct definition for each of the underlined words. Study the **context** *carefully before you choose your answer.*

1. "People who have the condition often are <u>adept</u> at hiding it. They resort to <u>elaborate</u> means to cover it up. That's understandable, since there is still a large <u>stigma</u> attached to it." (lines 10–14)

   <u>adept</u>:   A. inexperienced   B. highly skilled   C. adequate

   <u>elaborate</u>:   A. very careful, thorough   B. expensive   C. obvious

   <u>stigma</u>:   A. sign of shame   B. sign of poverty   C. sign of stupidity

2. "He was still <u>pondering</u> his list and looking at the spices on the shelf, trying to match the writing on the list with the writing on the packages he saw." (lines 47–50)

   <u>pondering</u>:   A. scanning   B. slowly reading   C. carefully examining

3. "When he made a selection, he seemed so unsure. His cart was filling up awfully slowly. I could imagine his <u>frustration</u>." (lines 60–63)

   <u>frustration</u>:   A. anger   B. discouragement   C. anxiety

4. "But I knew the wonderful new world that being able to read would open up to him. It would surely make his life less complicated. He wouldn't have to <u>pretend</u> anymore." (lines 74–77)

   <u>pretend</u>:   A. act falsely   B. be ashamed   C. be truthful

What are the qualifications for a President of the United States? What are the seven basic roles of the President? What does the 22nd Amendment to the Constitution provide? These and other questions about the presidency are answered in the following excerpt from The World Book, *an encyclopedia. An encyclopedia is a book or a set of books containing information on a wide range of subjects or on all aspects of one subject.*

The President of the United States is often considered the most powerful elected official in the world. The President leads a nation of great wealth and military strength. Presidents have often provided de-
5 cisive leadership in times of crisis, and they have shaped many important events in history.

The Constitution of the United States gives the President enormous power. However, it also limits that power. The authors of the Constitution wanted
10 a strong leader as President, but they did not want an all-powerful king. As a result, they divided the powers of the United States government among three branches—executive, legislative, and judicial. The President, who is often called the *chief executive,*
15 heads the executive branch. Congress represents the legislative branch. The Supreme Court of the United States and other federal courts make up the judicial

President of the United States

from THE WORLD BOOK

branch. Congress and the Supreme Court may prevent or end any presidential action that exceeds the
20 limits of the President's powers and trespasses on their authority.

The President has many roles and performs many duties. As chief executive, the President makes sure that federal laws are enforced. As commander in chief
25 of the nation's armed forces, the President is responsible for national defense. As foreign policy director, the President determines United States relations with other nations. As legislative leader, the President recommends new laws and works to win their
30 passage. As head of a political party, the President helps mold the party's positions on national and foreign issues. As popular leader, the President tries to inspire the American people to work together to meet the nation's goals. Finally, as chief of state,

35 the President performs a large variety of ceremonial duties.

. . .

The Presidency

Legal Qualifications. The Constitution establishes only three qualifications for a President. A President must (1) be at least 35 years old, (2) have lived in
40 the United States 14 years, and (3) be a natural-born citizen. The courts have never decided whether a person born abroad to American parents could serve as President, but many scholars believe such a person would be considered a natural-born citizen.

45 *Term of Office.* The President is elected to a four-year term. The 22nd Amendment to the Constitution provides that no one may be elected President more than twice. Nobody who has served as President for more than two years of someone else's term may be
50 elected more than once. Before the 22nd Amendment was approved in 1951, a President could serve an unlimited number of terms. Franklin D. Roosevelt held office longest. He was elected four times and served from March 1933 until his death in April 1945.
55 President William H. Harrison served the shortest time in office. He died a month after his inauguration in 1841.

The Constitution allows Congress to remove a President from office. The President first must be
60 *impeached* (charged with wrong-doing) by a majority vote of the House of Representatives. Then, the Senate, with the chief justice of the United States serving as presiding officer, tries the President on the charges. Removal from office requires conviction* by a two-
65 thirds vote of the Senate. Only one President, Andrew Johnson, has been impeached. He remained in office, however, because the Senate failed to convict him of the charges.

Salary and Other Allowances. The President receives a salary of $200,000 a year. The chief executive also gets $50,000 annually for expenses,

---

* *convict:* to find (someone) guilty in a court of law

plus allowances for staff, travel, and maintenance of the White House. Congress establishes all these amounts.

75 After leaving office, a President qualifies for a pension of about $99,500 yearly. Other retirement benefits include allowances for office space, staff, and mailing expenses. Widowed spouses of former Presidents get an annual pension of $20,000.

. . .

80 *The Inauguration* is the ceremony of installing the new or reelected President in office. It is held at noon on January 20 after the election. Up to 100,000 spectators attend the inauguration, which usually takes place outside the U.S. Capitol in Washington, 85 D.C. Millions of other Americans see the event on television.

The highlight occurs when the new President takes the oath of office from the chief justice of the United States. With right hand raised and left hand on an 90 open Bible, the new President says: "I do solemnly swear (or affirm) that I will faithfully execute the

office of President of the United States, and will to the best of my ability, preserve, protect, and defend the Constitution of the United States."

. . .

95 *Guarding the President.* The United States Secret Service guards the President at all times. In addition, agents of the Secret Service continually check the President's food, surroundings, and travel arrangements.

100 At various times, the President travels in an official car, a private airplane, or a U.S. Navy ship. The chief executive usually flies long distances in a reserved jet called *Air Force One.*

Even though U.S. Presidents get tight protection, 105 four chief executives have been assassinated while in office. They were Abraham Lincoln in 1865, James Garfield in 1881, William McKinley in 1901, and John F. Kennedy in 1963. Others have survived attempted assassinations, including Harry S. Truman, 110 Gerald R. Ford, and Ronald Reagan.

THE FAMILY CIRCUS   **by Bill Keane**

Copyright 1977,
The Register and Tribune
Syndicate, Inc.

"They're encyclopedias — in case we need to know something and Mommy isn't here."

Reading Comprehension

Answer the following questions.

1. The President of the United States is one of the most powerful elected officials in the world, yet his power is limited. The last part of the preceding statement seems to contradict* the first. Explain the statement.
2. Ronald Reagan, former actor, had roles in a number of movies; explain "roles" in this context. As President of the United States, Ronald Reagan had many roles; explain "roles" in this context. Give several examples.
3. Dr. Henry Kissinger, a naturalized citizen of the United States, taught at Harvard University from 1957 to 1969. He served as Secretary of State under Presidents Nixon and Ford from 1973 to 1977. Many people think he would make an excellent President of the United States. Is he legally qualified?
4. What do you think brought about the approval of the 22nd Amendment?
5. To impeach a President means to remove him from office. True or false? Explain your answer.
6. Who decides how much salary a President receives? Do Mrs. Carter and Mrs. Reagan receive annual pensions of $20,000? Explain your answer.
7. Are a Presidential inauguration and a Presidential election the same? Explain your answer.
8. Why does the Secret Service check the President's food? Who was the most recent President involved in an assassination attempt?

---

* *contradict:* to be opposite to

Personal ads have become popular in the United States as a means of meeting people of the opposite sex. Ads like the following appear in many newspapers and magazines throughout the country. Caution: Meeting people through personal ads can be dangerous.

1 ARE you SWM 30-42, 5'9" or taller, athletic, intelligent? A slim SWF, attractive, blonde, seeks fun, excitement & lasting relationship. Photo. P 1329 Journal-Constitution.

2 ATTRACTIVE, warm, sincere, caring, DWCF. Seeks sincere male 59-70. I like music, travel, camping, mtns, beach. Tell me about your likes. Send letter, photo. P 1325 Journal-Constitution.

3 DWM, handsome fin. sec. Germ-Amer, very caring, sport teacher 6', looking for petite, slender, sexy 25-40 white female. No games, no drugs. P 1377 Journal-Constitution.

4 DWM seeks DWF 39-49 for quality relationship. I am professional good manners, love white wine, conversation, interesting women. Note, will respond.
P 1340 JOURNAL-CONSTITUTION

5 DWM, 34, attractive, active, stable, single dad, seeks WF 30-36, attractive, non-smoker for low pressure, fun relationship, Fayetteville area. Note/photo plz.
p 1349 Journal-Constitution

Let's Get Personal

6 DWM 34, 5'9", 140, would like to meet female 25-35, who likes children, fitness, home life, nonsmoker, tired of rat race, send photo/phone in letter.
P 1420 JOURNAL-CONSTITUTION

7 DWM 58 seeks WF 53-58 for lasting relationship, sincere only! Possible marriage. If you are looking for ball-room dancing, moonlite bays, travels, concerts, arts, theatre, ballet, sugar daddy, Don't Answer This Ad!
P 1348 JOURNAL-CONSTITUTION

8 HONEST, sincere, professional, SWM 25, seeks SWF 21-30 to share a bottle of wine, a quiet candle light dinner, backpacking in the mountains, dancing til dawn, or any other romantic idea we can come up with. Take a chance!
P 1327 Journal-Constitution

9 HOT LANTA! Where are you? SWM 29 "Blue eyed cutie" I travel a lot-find it hard to meet another cutie! Pls. send note w/photo & phone.
P 1330 Journal-Constitution.

10 If you are a trim, attractive, sensuous lady 30-45 and can handle spending the rest of your life with a handsome successful executive 53 in the N. GA Mountains, please respond to:
P 1382 Journal-Constitution

11 WWF 60 Seeks WWM 60–67, out-going, neat, honest, caring, dances, movies or quiet nights at home. Note; Ph. P 1401 Journal-Constitution.

12 YOUNG MAN (23) in England (UK) wants American Pen-Friends, photo appreciated. P 1438 Journal-Constitution.

13 PHYSICIAN DWM 49, 5'8", 165 lbs, sensitive, attractive, fit, seeks SWF 34-45. Must be college grad. Articulate, cult. sophisticated, slim, attractive, who enjoys symphony, sports, plays, world travel & good conversation. Send recent photo-phone No. & note.
P 1339 JOURNAL-CONSTITUTION.

14 PRETTY SBF, indep. 39, slender, new to Atl. Seeks SBM, tall, attractive, 35-45 for dating, poss. relationship. Phone-photo-note please. P 1333 Journal-Constitution.

15 SBF, 30, 5'5", 120 lbs, attractive and well-educated. Seeks SBM with similar qualities, age 30-33 for romance. P 1332 Journal-Constitution.

16 SINCERE professional, straight, attractive SWM, seeks discreet attractive, loving WF under 45. Must enjoy cozy romantic eves.
P 1384 JOURNAL-CONSTITUTION

17 SUCCESSFUL SJM professional seeks SJF age 23-33 under 5'7", non-smoking to share good times and good life. Phone & photo appreciated.
P 1345 JOURNAL-CONSTITUTION

18 SUMMER Clearance, limited edition 1957 SWM in mint condition, low mileage, loaded, clean, unlimited warranty, must see to appreciate. Make best offer. Photo and note please. Photos returned.
P 1331 Journal-Constitution.

19 SWF 27 beautiful desires arrangement with WM 35-55. I am expensive but worth it. Send telephone & photo. P 1326 Journal-Constitution.

20 SWM—Nice looking, secure. Professional, stable—5'9", 185 lbs, 41 yrs., no children. Looking for SWF 25-40 yrs, intelligent, trim, attractive, to share dinners, travel, boating, adventures, and other activities. Please send response and photo if possible. All serious replies will be answered. P 1013 Journal-Constitution.

21 SWM-wants female dancing partner, friend, lover. Athletic—5'10", chest 43, waist 34, solid 170 lbs, healthy, computer tech., a yankee doodle dandy. P 1380 JOURNAL-CONSTITUTION

22 SWM, 31, 5'11", 185 lbs, sincere, non-smoker, never married, excellent physical condition. Seeks S/DWF 25-32 with no children, professional, athletic, career minded, self assured & looking for a lasting relationship. Recent photo & letter. P1427, C/O Journal/Constitution.

23 SWM 42, attractive, prof. 6'1, 175, brown hair/eyes, sincere, honest. Enjoy outdoors, water sports, movies or quiet night at home. Seeking S/DWF 32-42 for honest relationship. Photo & note please.
P 1356 Journal-Constitution.

24 W Asian M, 35, 5'8", 145 lbs. Seeks an educated sincere. Two kinds or little over weight ok. Send photo and phone Number. P 1381 Journal-Constitution.

25 WM Generous Executive 54, 5'10", 160 lbs seeks F in Augusta-Milledgeville-Athens area for relationship. Advise when and where to meet or Tele. No. P1459 Journal-Constitution.

26 WHAT A Waste uncommon very attractive 5'6, slim athletic sophisticated, intelligent, educated, well traveled, sincere & caring European Woman forced by a recent personal tragedy into a lonely changed life style. Would like to meet cultured well educated Prof., tall good looking 48-62 well traveled, kind hearted healthy & generous, to have an unusual friend. No Commitment required.
P 1442 Journal-Constitution

27 DWM 42, 5'6", 130 lbs, honest, settled, warm and caring, seeks S/DWF who is slim, attractive and interested in a meaningful relationship. 25 to 45. Phone and photo.
P 1344 Journal-Constitution

28 SWM, 27, 6'2", 185 lbs, recently transferred to Atlanta. Seek SWF to explore the city with. Enjoy travel, outdoors, new experiences. Pls provide photo/phone.
P 1417 JOURNAL-CONSTITUTION

29 ADVENTUROUS, affectionate, attractive, profes., petite SWF, 31, seeking humorous, handsome, honest, fit, SWM, non-smoker. Photo/note. P 1418 Journal-Constitution.

30 MIGRAINE HEADACHES—I need your help for my family. If you have a personal cure for your headache please send info. to: P.O. Box 5601, Rome, Ga. 30161.

31 ATTRACTIVE SWM 35, Banker seeks, D/SWF 25-45 to share the autumn mountains and quiet dinners.
P 1414 JOURNAL-CONSTITUTION

32 GENEROUS WM, seeks girl of his dreams. Busty WF Morganaor patron type for discreet relationship. Send recent photo, ph, note.
P 1421 JOURNAL-CONSTITUTION

33 ATTRACTIVE female wants to meet same for fun and friendship. Send note with photo and phone.
P 1350 JOURNAL-CONSTITUTION

34 WF 30, 115, pretty, seeks M, 20-37 for discreet friendship & fun. Send note, photo & phone number, P 1444 Journal-Constitution.

35 MILLIONAIRE ATLANTA EXEC. NEW to town. Single, athletic Male 5'7", 40ish with a Regal Cat, lacks the one ingredient in my dynamic lifestyle - an educated articulate woman with class, charm, femininity and sophistication. I like spectator sports, running, racquetball, bridge, chess, T.V., movies, reading and good conversation and enjoy all the amenities resulting from my success: flexible schedule, penthouse, Mercedes, national & international travel.
If you are a slender, Non Smoking attractive, well educated, 30ish Woman who truly enjoys the opposite sex & share some of my interests, let's meet for lunch/drink. Detailed letter & photo helpful. Ad No 1313 C/O Journal-Constitution, P.O. Box 4689, Atlanta, Ga 30302

Reading Comprehension

Answer the following questions.

1. What do the following letters stand for?

   SWM   _Single White Male_ _____

   SWF   _____

   SBF   _____

   DWM   _____

   WWF   _____

   DWCF   _____

2. According to the personal ads, what *physical attributes* do men find attractive in women, and vice versa*?

3. What *personal qualities* are men seeking in women, and vice versa?

4. Can you infer from the ads that people are health conscious? Explain.

5. In ad 18, the SWM has a good sense of humor. How do you know?

6. Why do you think it can be dangerous to meet people through personal ads? How do people in your country find new friends?

_____

* *vice versa:* opposite of what was previously stated (*women* find attractive in *men*)

Vocabulary

MEANING FROM CONTEXT

In the following sentences, try to guess the meaning of each <u>underlined</u> word or phrase from its **context.**

1. Children need <u>stable</u> parents—parents whom they can always depend on.

   stable (ad 5): _____

2. He decided to get out of the <u>rat race</u> and lead a slower, less confusing, and more purposeful life.

   rat race (ad 6): _____

3. Anita's <u>sugar daddy</u> was a lot older than she, but he gave her diamonds, beautiful clothes, and expensive cars.

   sugar daddy (ad 7): _____

4. Many <u>straights</u> are prejudiced against gays.

   straights (ad 16): _____

5. "I . . . enjoy all the <u>amenities</u> resulting from my success: flexible schedule, penthouse, Mercedes, national and international travel."

   amenities (ad 35): _____

Activity: Writing Personal Ads

Pretend you want to meet someone of the opposite sex. Write your own personal ad.

_____

_____

_____

_____

_____

_____

_____

_____

_____

_____

_____

_____

The following is an excerpt from Our Marvelous Native Tongue, *a history of the English language by Robert Claiborne.*

The total number of English words lies somewhere between 400,000—the number of current entries in the largest English dictionaries—and 600,000—the largest figure that any expert is willing to be quoted
5 on.* By comparison, the biggest French dictionaries have only about 150,000 entries, the biggest Russian ones a mere 130,000.

* According to McCrum, Cran, and MacNeil in *The Story of English,* "The . . . *Oxford English Dictionary* lists about 500,000 words; and a further half million technical and scientific terms remain uncatalogued."

Our uncertainty over the size of the English vocabulary arises in part out of a longtime propensity
10 among English speakers for making the same "word" serve several different functions. Thus "love" means something we feel, but also something we do—not to mention a zero score in tennis; do we count it as one word, or two, or three? Then, do slang words
15 count, or dialect terms? If we include scientific and technical terms, most of them used by only a small percentage of English speakers, what about the special jargons and lingoes of various trades and subcultures: the newspaperman's "sidebar" (a subsidiary
20 story running alongside the main story) . . . or the physician's "i.v." (intravenous) injection?

But no matter how one reckons up the numbers, the total is enormous. Of course, bigger isn't always better; often it is a good deal worse. Words, on the

The Importance of Speaking English

by ROBERT CLAIBORNE

25 other hand, are a kind of natural resource; it is impossible to have too many of them. Not, indeed, that any one of us will ever get around to using more than a fraction of our enormous thesaurus** ("treasury"—from Greek) of words, not least because tens
30 of thousands of them are intelligible only to specialists. But even the fraction in general use endows us with a uniquely rich assortment of synonyms on almost any subject under the sun: words that mean more or less the same thing, yet each of which pos-
35 sesses its own special qualities of sound and rhythm and shade of meaning . . . .

Consider merely one category of our words, verbs, and one subdivision of those: the verbs that deal with the everyday activities of eating, sleeping, working

** *thesaurus:* also a book of synonyms and antonyms

40 and playing. At table, we may eat, devour, consume, munch, nibble or gulp our food; if we then feel overstuffed, we may doze, nap, snooze, sleep, slumber or nod off. In factory or office or down on the farm, we work, labor, toil, drudge or slave at our
45 appointed tasks—though we may sometimes loaf, laze, dog it or goof off. When the whistle blows, we play, sport, revel, make merry or amuse ourselves, some of us with drinking, tippling, boozing, carousing, wetting our whistles, bending an elbow or tying
50 one on. And if, perchance, we find the strain of all this activity, linguistic and otherwise, too much to take, we may go crazy, mad or insane; wax lunatic; crack up; go berserk or run amok—not to speak of flipping out, going bananas or suffering a nervous
55 breakdown . . . .

It is the enormous and variegated lexicon of English, far more than the mere numbers and geographical spread of its speakers, that truly makes our native tongue marvelous—makes it, in fact, a medium for
60 the precise, vivid and subtle expression of thought and emotion that has no equal, past or present.

At this point, some readers will suspect me of exaggeration if not outright cultural chauvinism. Can I really be claiming that English is not merely a great
65 language but the greatest? Yes, that is exactly what I'm saying—and I don't consider myself any sort of chauvinist.

Whether any culture can be shown to be "better" overall than any other is doubtful. But it is a matter
70 of historical record that certain cultures have been better *at certain things* than others. For example, between 1814 and 1914, England and America produced some able painters—yet would anyone seriously compare them with French artists of the same
75 period, not to mention the great Dutchmen of the seventeenth century, or the great Italians of the fourteenth to sixteenth centuries? Between 1650 and 1900, the German-speaking peoples produced half a dozen top-rank composers and as many second-rank
80 ones, while England has not had a major composer since Handel (d. 1759)—and *he* was a German! Anyone with even a modest knowledge of cultural history could easily cite a dozen more examples.

If all these peoples have made their own remark-
85 able, even unique cultural contributions, it doesn't
seem to me chauvinistic to credit the English-speak-
ing peoples with their own unique achievements.

And one of these, surely, is our English tongue, along
with the rich heritage of prose, poetry and drama it
90 has helped create.

Reading Comprehension

TRUE/FALSE STATEMENTS

Answer the following statements True or False.

_____ 1. There are perhaps one million words in the English language.

_____ 2. Jargon is the specialized or technical language of a trade, profession, or similar group.

_____ 3. "Sidebar" is computer jargon.

_____ 4. "Bigger is better" describes how the author feels about the vocabulary of a language.

_____ 5. Mr. Claiborne states that English is a marvelous language because it is spoken by millions of people throughout the world.

_____ 6. The author claims that some cultures are superior to others.

QUESTIONS AND DISCUSSION

Answer the following questions.

1. Give several reasons why experts are uncertain about the size of the English vocabulary.
2. How much of the vast English vocabulary is in general use and why? Why are those words in general use considered special by the author?
3. Why does Mr. Claiborne believe that English is the greatest language in the world? Define "cultural chauvinism." Why does the author say he is not a cultural chauvinist?

Vocabulary

SYNONYMS

Part 1

There are few perfect synonyms. Look at the synonyms below that mean to *chew and swallow food*. Are their meanings identical? Can one be substituted for another in a sentence without changing the effect of the sentence?

eat

consume
devour
dine
gobble
gorge
sup
wolf

These words refer to the partaking of food. **Eat** is the most general, applying equally well to man or animal: the woman *eating* a hot dog; horses *eating* fodder. Only context can give further details: slowly *eating* his breakfast of hot chocolate and croissants; *eating* his bowl of soup almost in one gulp. **Dine** and **sup** are relatively formal; both specifically refer to *eating* done by people. *Dine* can point to the day's main meal: She *ate* a light lunch so that she would be able to *dine* later without a guilty conscience. Or the word can refer to any formal or special meal: She asked her husband's employer to *dine* with them next week. *Sup* now sounds archaic and, worse, pretentious, though once it could refer to an evening or late evening meal: They had a nightcap and *supped* on leftovers once the guests were gone.

Unlike the preceding pair, **consume** can refer to either man or animal, but its point in either case is the thoroughness of the *eating,* suggesting the utter and avid taking in of a food: a pack of lions able to *consume* the whole carcass of an impala in a single night; The hungry boy *consumed* every last scrap on his plate. Thus, the word can apply to any process that involves total destruction and in which one thing can be seen as feeding off another: the raging fever that was *consuming* her body. **Gorge** compares to *consume,* but stresses *eating* or even overeating to the point of satiety or possibly discomfort, suggesting the gluttonous and indiscriminate stuffing down of food: the sleepy hounds lying about *gorged* with food; the fat man who *gorged* himself constantly with mountainous desserts.

Gobble emphasizes rapid *eating* rather than the thoroughness indicated by *consume* or the excessiveness possible for *gorge*: chickens who *gobbled* down the scattered bread-crumbs in a twinkling; He warned the girl that she'd get sick if she *gobbled* her food that way. **Wolf** also emphasizes quickness, but it indicates a ravenous ferocity or desperation, as well. Since its obvious metaphor pertaining to one animal might make the word tautological in that instance and inappropriate in others, the main point of the word is to describe human *eating* in terms of a wolf's swift and rapacious feeding: *wolfing* down one canape after another as though he was starving; a movie that depicted Henry VIII *wolfing* down an incredible array of viands.

Devour can apply equally well to animals or men, though it is more general in its implications than the preceding, suggesting either the total consumption of something or the rapidity with which it is eaten: kittens that *devoured* the whole plate of catfood before the dozing mother cat could stir; hungry soldiers who *devoured* the tasteless creamed beef ladled out to them by the mess sergeant. Like *consume,* this word can have metaphorical uses, referring in this case to eager or enthusiastic taking in or, possibly, to the predatory destruction of something. [She *devoured* her French lessons so that she would be proficient by the time of her first trip abroad; All their assets were *devoured* by an unscrupulous loan shark.] See ABSORB.

How do the sentences below differ in meaning although the <u>underlined</u> words are all **synonyms** *of* **eat?**

1. Lillian and her friends <u>dined</u> and then went to the theater.
2. Lillian and her friends <u>gobbled</u> their dinner and then went to the theater.
3. Lillian and her friends <u>gorged</u> themselves and then went to the theater.
4. Lillian and her friends <u>nibbled</u> at their dinner and then went to the theater.

Part 2

List as many **synonyms** *as you can think of for the word* **beautiful.** *How do they differ in meaning?*

_____   _____

_____   _____

_____   _____

_____   _____

What is the **antonym** *for these words?*

_____